Warsaw

TOPOGRAPHICS

Warsaw

David Crowley

REAKTION BOOKS

For Edith, Noah and Lily

Published by Reaktion Books Ltd
79 Farringdon Road, London EC1M 3JU

www.reaktionbooks.co.uk

First published 2003

Printed and bound in Great Britain by
Cromwell Press, Trowbridge, Wiltshire

British Library Cataloguing in Publication Data:
Crowley, David
    Warsaw. – (Topographics)
    1. Architecture – Poland – Warsaw – 20th century.
    2. Warsaw (Poland) – Description and travel 3. Warsaw (Poland) –
    Social Life and customs – 20th century 4. Warsaw (Poland) –
    Civilization – 20th century 5. Warsaw (Poland) – Intellectual life –
    20th century
    I. Title
    943.8'4'09045

ISBN 1 86189 179 2

Contents

Audience waiting for a performance of Andrzej Wajda's *The Supper* in the ruined church on Żytnia Street in the early 1990s.

Introduction

Visiting Warsaw from London in the 1990s I was invariably asked by friends living there, 'How much has the city changed?' and 'What's new here?' That people passing the construction sites and struggling to move through streets congested with new cars every day of the week should ask these questions of a visitor seemed strange. It was as if the sensation of change was more pronounced if experienced *staccato* rather than *glissando*. Encouraged to feel they were experiencing History in the making – the end of a 'great social experiment' – my Warsaw friends wanted more palpable evidence of change *as change*. They were keen to relay which streets had been renamed, some finding a satisfyingly ironic charge in the rededication of a street once named after a 'hero of labour' to Jerzy Popiełuszko, a priest murdered by the Secret Police in 1984. They pointed out the new skyscrapers (though one hardly needs directions to find these new spires) and the 'privatization' of other public landmarks: the squat Communist Party headquarters transformed into the stock exchange or spaces in the towering Palace of Culture and Science made into a casino.[1]

In 2000 they also encouraged me to come to an exhibition in Warsaw's Zachęta Gallery and, more importantly, to witness the crowds of people queuing to see it. Entitled 'Szare w kolorze, 1956–1970. Kultura okresu gomułkowskiego' (Grey in Colour, 1956–1970. Culture from the Gomułka Era), this show resurrected the more colourful aspects of life from the 1960s. The high and ornate spaces in this major art centre, better known for its display of works by artists on the international circuit, were transformed into rooms representing ordinary, cramped flats in the apartment blocks from the 1950s and '60s. Other spaces recreated the small private galleries that first showed abstract paintings after the straightjacket of Socialist Realism was thrown off in the mid-1950s as well as the dimly lit student clubs where serious young men in suits and hand-painted ties once played loud jazz. A cinema showed comedy and film noir movies from the period to a packed auditorium. However, the most popular recreation – at least to judge from the authentically long queue – was an interior of a 'milk bar' (*bar mleczny*), the traditional canteen found in every Polish town where students and workers could eat a cheap and often tasteless meal. These diners were notorious for the shabbiness of their décor and even shabbier service. Food stewing in vats would be delivered through a hole in the wall by a taciturn cook. The exhibition's curators created an accurate copy of the original, even to the extent of serving food to visitors. Nostalgia among the visitors to the show was prompted as much by visceral smells and tastes as high-brow sights. Just as Proust's remembrance of things past was triggered by a 'Madeleine' biscuit consumed over tea with his aunt, the clatter of cheap cutlery and the taste of over-cooked dumplings seemed to have a similar sentimental effect.

The appeal of this unexpectedly popular exhibition was that it represented a disappearing world within the compass of memory. So rapid has been the turn of events that the material world of the recent past has already acquired an exotic otherness. In fact, some of the things under the gallery's spotlight can still be found – often decaying and overlooked – in the streets outside. No conservationists are lobbying to keep the neon signs that once illuminated Polish towns with smiling cows promoting the state dairy or with racing motorcyclists encouraging sales of tickets in the national lottery. High-rise housing blocks and milk bars are not about to be listed as part of the architectural heritage. The exhibition revealed a desire to remember the contours of everyday life in 'Peerel',[2] albeit within limits. After all, no one was arguing for the resurrection of this world. And safely within the confines of the gallery, it offered no resistance to processes erasing the traces of socialism from the city.

This exhibition was part of the wide-ranging search for the sensation of change; to be certain that was then and this is now. There has, after all, been a strong ideological 'need' – both within Poland and without – to emphasize it. Former communists are keen to demonstrate that they have been born again as democrats. Western commentators, particularly those reporting to the business class investing in the Polish economy, celebrate the transformation of Poland from a destitute socialist society to a vigorous capitalist market. While change may be inevitable and even necessary in public life, it can be unsettling when viewed through the prism of personal experience. After all, the success of the 'Grey in Colour' exhibition was largely due to the way that it captured ordinary and yet moving sensations – the excitement of furnishing a new flat after living in a cramped workers' hostel; the powerful effect of seeing a modern painting or an evocative film for the first time; or of buying a fashionably printed dress on the city's street markets. While these and many other experiences occurred in a socialist society, they were not exclusively defined by it.

That Poland and Warsaw, in particular, has changed there is no doubt. But changefulness is, after all, what characterizes urban life. Those cities that fail to change stagnate. And cities that insist on preservation or conservation make a statement about the value of the past in and over the present. Warsaw has felt the sweep of such pressures in the period surveyed by this book from the end of the Second World War to the twenty-first century. This book explores the forces encouraging and inhibiting change in the fabric of the city during the rise and decline of socialism and its dismantling after 1989. It explores the effects of the weight of the past, both imagined and material, on the way that the city has been remade, particularly in the 1950s and again in the 1990s. It also measures the pulses of modernization that sought to improve streets, homes and shops.

If change is a general and defining characteristic of modern life and the modern city, as it surely is, state socialism directed it in particular ways. Marxism-Leninism, the ideology to which authority subscribed before 1989, took change as its raison d'être. Not only did it envisage the future, it sought to speed its arrival. The changes that occurred in Warsaw, socialism's greatest project in post-war Poland, were to be greater here than anywhere else. As we'll see, Warsaw was even to have its own 'tempo', such was the pace of change on its streets. However, ideology is never the mirror of reality. In the intervals between dramas like the de-Stalinizing 'Thaw' in the mid-1950s and the rise of Solidarność (Solidarity) in 1980, there were long periods when time seemed to drag. This was an everyday sensation, experienced watching the hands of a clock tick in the queue for food in the corner store or one's name move slowly up the waiting list for an apartment. Warsaw's 'tempo' slowed too. New buildings took years to be completed while architects and construction workers combined their 'official' jobs with work on the informal economy (or queued outside the city's shops). Buildings were not renovated or improved. Many of the bright, modern cafes and shops built during the 1950s – and symptoms of the optimism that many felt after the Stalinists fell from power – were unchanged at the end of the System and lent the city an oddly quaint appearance. The Hotel Bristol, a tall and elegant neo-Renaissance style structure dating from 1901 on Krakowskie Przedmieście, Warsaw's Allee unter den Linden, was one of the rare buildings to survive the assault on the city in 1944. First used for high-powered Party meetings in the 1950s, it slipped into disrepair, becoming the haunt of students from nearby Warsaw University. Closed after flooding in 1981, it was boarded up and became a building site that seemed to display few signs of work for more than a decade. Warsaw conserved its features – like a neglected time capsule – because the governing classes lacked the resources and the drive to change and renew its fabric.

The cycle of stagnation and growth experienced in the People's Republic was not new to Warsaw. It had been the city's fate for much of the nineteenth century. Stripped of its status as royal seat and site of the national parliament when Poland was partitioned for the third and final time by her neighbouring states in 1795, Warsaw was reduced to a provincial town. Under Prussian rule, tariffs and new custom duties stifled trade and the city's population halved. Hopes for revival, first raised by the arrival of Napoleon's troops in Warsaw in 1806, were more substantially realized after the Congress of Vienna in 1815 when the Congress Kingdom was established. The city, though now dependent on Russia, experienced an economic and cultural boom that made a lasting impression on its fabric and its self-image. Numerous residences, public and municipal buildings were constructed in neo-classical dress including the Bank of Poland on Plac Bankowy, the National Theatre and the Staszic Palace, home to the Society of the Friends of Sciences. In an era of self-conscious modernization, the city was cleared of some of its medieval structures: the city walls and gates were pulled down to allow the extension of the Castle Square (Plac Zamkowy).

Polish desires for reunification and national sovereignty were not satisfied by what is traditionally referred to by the diminutive 'Kongresówka': The Congress Kingdom was a political compromise that left the Polish cities of Kraków and Poznań outside its borders. With the Tsar as the King of Poland, Warsaw became the centre of conspiracy that climaxed in the unsuccessful uprisings of 1830–31 and 1863–4. Following each, the authorities punished Warsaw with executions, exile and martial law. In 1831 Tsar Nicholas I's troops

confiscated and destroyed 136 residences – large and small – in Żoliborz, a green suburb to the north of the city, to clear the ground for
the construction of the huge Alexander Citadel, which was to function as barracks, prison and execution ground. While Warsaw came
to enjoy many of the technologies stimulating urban expansion elsewhere, including the arrival of the first railway in 1847 (a symbolic
moment in the history of most cities), growth was limited by a military ban on construction in the vicinity of the Citadel and the fortifications encircling the city. Such strictures – in place until 1911 –
contributed to the terrible overcrowding and homelessness in a city
with a rapidly increasing population (drawing close to one million
just before the outbreak of the First World War).[3]

In the words of one historian, Russia's 'increasingly moribund
ruling elite … turned Warsaw into a grotesquely enormous military
fortress but equally one of the most significant railway junctions of
the day'.[4] For Russia, Warsaw was both a troublesome garrison city
on the edge of Empire and, at the same time, a crucial point of contact with the rest of Europe (in a literal sense, for this was where
cargo on Russia's wide-gauge trains was unloaded onto Europe's
narrower wagons to continue its journey west). Warsaw's commer-
cially strategic location stimulated considerable raggle-taggle development in the vicinity of Marszałkowska Street in the late nineteenth
century in the form of hotels, department stores, banks, factories and
market halls. A handful of these buildings were impressive, most
were shoddily constructed, exploiting lax building regulations.

After the 1860s the authorities extended their programme of
Russification of the Poles to the historic fabric of the city.[5] First taken
over by the Tsarist educational authorities in the aftermath of the
November Uprising of 1830, the Staszic Palace, for instance, was
stripped of its elegant neo-classical forms at the end of the century
and remodelled in the Byzantine-Russian style with elaborate poly-
chromatic tiles and an onion-domed spire. It then functioned as an
Orthodox chapel and Russian secondary school for boys. At the
same time, historic districts like the Old Town – significant places in
the national consciousness – fell into neglect. The merchants'
houses in the streets around the Rynek (Market Square) lost their
gilded elegance, becoming rookeries. Antoni Słonimski recalled
'small tenement homes full of dirt and foul smells where more than
a dozen people would live in a single apartment. These bug-ridden
flats lacked baths and even running water.'[6] The contrast between

11

dazzling imperial monuments and decaying Polish landmarks made Warsaw feel its subjugation all the more strongly.

When Poland achieved independence at the end of the First World War, the legacy of imperial rule to the city included over-crowding, poor communications (the Vistula bridges destroyed by the retreating Russian army in 1915), chaotic commercial develop-ment and Tsarist monuments.[7] Although the economic circum-stances in which the Second Republic found itself after 1918 were hardly propitious, the challenge of making a modern city capable of representing and governing the country engaged the minds of architects and politicians alike. New public buildings like the Sejm (Parliament, 1927–8) and the Muzeum Narodowe (National Museum, 1926–38), as well as the ritual demolition of Tsarist monu-ments like the colossal Alexander Nevsky Orthodox church in 1924–6, were predictable symbols of independence. New housing schemes and urban planning strategies in the 1930s suggested a more vigorous engagement with modernity. Żoliborz, a district once constrained by its proximity to the Citadel, was extended by a series of housing estates constructed by the Warszawska Spółdziel-nia Mieszkaniowa (Warsaw Housing Co-operative) from 1931. A number of central Modern Movement concepts were tested such as the 'existenzminimum' in its white-walled and flat-roofed apart-ment blocks.[8] The most powerful statement of faith in Warsaw's capacity to be modern was, however, an urban plan entitled 'Warszawa Funkcjonalna' (Functional Warsaw) produced by the architects Jan Chmielewski and Szymon Syrkus from 1931 to 1934. Emphasizing Warsaw's long history as a crossroads for trade and cultural exchange and its geomorphologic position (as well as their own intellectual orientation to internationalism), Chmielewski and Syrkus produced a city plan that extended, like a folded map, on a country-wide and even international scale. Rather than conceive the city in terms of fixed elements, 'Warszawa Funkcjonalna' envisaged the dissolution of city and national boundaries in an extensive network of road, rail and river routes and junctions.[9] Warsaw was not simply projected as a European city: it was to become Europe itself.

Conceiving the city in terms of movement, freed from the meta-physics of place, was, as Syrkus and Chmielewski acknowledged, a utopian dream. Cities are made by folding the new into the old. Urban textures are richer when traces and textures from different eras coexist and when the geomorphology of the location is exploited. Rarely does Warsaw compose itself into a picturesque arrangement of parts. The Vistula River running through the centre of city is unregulated, its wide sandy banks scattered with trees and tall clumps of reeds. Wild and beautiful, the river is an unexpected asset, yet, almost uniquely in Europe, the city turns its back on it. No major building faces the waterfront. Moreover, Warsaw often seems disjointed and disordered. Faltering patterns of economic development, dramatic reversals of ideology and the pendulum swings of history have left their mark. Different layers of urban form represent diverse allegiances and conflicting ideologies. From a rather more practical perspective, as we will see, the jarring contours of the city have rarely formed a neat 'fit' with the needs of the present (whether after 1918, 1945 or 1989).

Despite this, even the most banal remnants of the pre-war city are accorded high value today. Sensitivity to the presence of the past is, of course, most pronounced when its traces are under threat or have been lost. To walk south from the Old Town along Krakowskie Przedmieście in the knowledge its buildings and monuments, or the paving stones on which you tread, are not much more than fifty years old is an odd experience, such is their appearance of age. A recent architectural guide follows the historically correct procedure of dating all the buildings remade as historical facsimiles to the year of their reconstruction in the 1950s and '60s.[10] This information is rarely sufficient to correct the impression of one's eyes. In the centre, one comes upon voids and empty plots amongst the tenements, hotels and offices. Even without knowing what once stood on these sites, it is hard not to feel the sensation of absence. As I'll describe in the first chapter below, such presences and absences have strongly shaped the attachment that many people living in Warsaw feel for the city. The pre-war city has become the subject of waves of nostalgia that keeps many writers and publishers in business. And singers have had successful recording careers by adopting into their repertoire the tangos and ballads from working class districts like Praga and Powiśle. Illiterate and poorly housed, many residents of Warsaw would have found little in their experiences of the city to recommend it. But even the criminal gangs and poverty of the 1930s have been incorporated into a mythical Warsaw, cast as a world of tight-knit communities and colourful scoundrels, such is the appeal of the past.

This attachment, particularly to those traces of the past that survive in the present, stands in stark contrast to a perception of Warsaw that has had wide currency abroad. Viewed from London or Paris, the Polish capital is a place of drab and unrelenting concrete buildings on wide avenues constructed for military parades, and, as such, it is an index of the grey 'reality' of late Eastern Bloc socialism. This reading was lent emphasis by musicians like David Bowie and Joy Division (who in an early incarnation adopted the city's name) when they wanted to lend an austere charge to their doleful music. The subject of a peculiar form of exoticization, Warsaw had a perverse appeal as the site of a prolonged catastrophe.

While the Polish capital cannot be explored without understanding the effects of the war and Soviet-style socialism (or for that matter the debilitating consequences of Russian occupation in the nineteenth century), a city should not be conceived in terms of its misfortunes alone. Warsaw's emotional force lies in a wide range of ordinary experiences, relationships and attitudes that were shaped in the city. Above all, Warsaw was rebuilt by its citizens. Many people feel strongly that they (or their parents and grandparents) made the city. Warsaw was, in a much-repeated communist slogan, 'the people's city': this was the case in a particularly literal fashion. In 1945 ordinary Poles began clearing the streets of rubble by hand and burying the dead. They occupied the city's cellars and the few habitable buildings. Some historians have detected a kind of moral effect exerted by the resolution of ordinary people to restore these corners of the city.[11] While immediate post-war discussions were held in the corridors of power about moving the capital to Kraków, which had escaped destruction, or Łódź, a city of factories and workers with much stronger socialist bona-fides, authority, it seems, had little choice but to restore Warsaw's status.

Although not first to the starting blocks, the Party made conspicuous efforts to take the city as its prize. As I'll show, it claimed authorship of Warsaw's resurrection. This was an achievement, it stressed, that could only be realized with the organizational strategies and ideological drive of socialism. Yet Warsaw's revival to become a large and busy city – with picturesque narrow streets and churches at its heart, wide bridges spanning the wild banks of the Vistula, busy, dual lane thoroughfares and high-rise buildings – was and remains cause for widespread pride, even among those who rejected communist authority. This fact, one verging on paradox, occupies much of this book. Through a series of studies of different buildings and monuments in the city, I explore the effects of a rather allusive force before and after 1989, that of public opinion. Despite having the weight of the legal system at its disposal and Moscow on its back, the party-state sought popular endorsement, particularly in the sensitive case of commemorating the recent past. Although more effective mechanisms for gathering views are in place today, as we'll see, authority, in its diffuse forms, is not always more receptive to public sentiment.

Although this is a book about the city's streets, monuments, squares and alleys, her churches and her synagogues, it focuses little on artistic or architectural matters. It offers few insights into the creative imaginations of those who were responsible for the best (or worst) spaces in the city. In fact, post-war Warsaw is credited with few notes of architectural distinction. Registering highly on a scale of kitschness, the Stalin-era Palace of Culture and Science has had more attention from commentators than the numerous shops, public buildings and housing schemes that were designed and constructed with care and imagination from the 1940s. If Warsaw's urban make-up has attracted interest at all, it has usually been in terms of tragedy, as a city rebuilt from rubble and ashes.

The purpose of this book is rather different. It explores the way in which new and old spaces were represented and used by those who have claimed authority over the city since 1944, as well as the people who have lived and worked there. In this, I ask the following broad questions: Where and how was the past commemorated in the city? Where, for what and how did people shop? And where and how did they live? These are everyday matters. But that does not mean that they are without consequence. In a country that has been subject to the authority of Stalin's henchmen and the effects of the free-market in the span of little more than two generations, history, consumption and privacy have been highly charged fields that many have claimed to know best. Soviet-style socialism was, more than any other, an arrogant ideology promising to transform both the way that people live and their consciousness of the past, present and future. The city was not just a material reflection of these aims: it was to be a social transformer. It hardly needs to be said that Warsaw never came close to being the socialist city promised by the ideologues and planners in the 1950s. But it was, nevertheless, shaped by the experience of Eastern Bloc socialism. Its post-war monuments, shops and homes – rarely authentically 'Soviet' – reveal much about the changing ideological priorities and tactical operations of Polish socialism over the forty years to 1989. These spaces and buildings now constitute the material legacy of one system to another. While the new air-conditioned, glass towers that international corporations and property developers have built are invoked as symbols of change, they are not its index. Ordinary, and often overlooked, Warsaw's monuments, shops and homes have far more to tell.

1 Monuments in Ruins

The poet Miron Białoszewski witnessed terrible events in Warsaw during the Second World War. A young man, he sought sanctuary in the cellars of the Old Town while the occupying German forces destroyed the city above. His escape route to safety was, like that of many, through the network of dank sewers. Some twenty-five years later, he published a book with the matter-of-fact title *Pamiętnik z Powstania Warszawskiego* (A Memoir of the Warsaw Uprising). Reflecting on the ill-fated uprising against Nazi control of the city in 1944 – an ever-popular, even overbearing theme in Polish history writing – Białoszewski's descriptions are uncertain. He was both an eyewitness and an eloquent writer, yet his prose is punctured with hesitation. His frequent use of words like 'perhaps', 'I think' and 'maybe' unsettle the reader who wants to know what happened in the besieged city. In his hesitancy, Białoszewski seems to ask: do I really recall? Are my memories *my* memories? His book is, as he stresses, not a work of History written to 'play the sage' but an attempt to direct and narrate the incendiary discharges of his memory.[1] In one passage describing the life-saving network of sewers, Białoszewski seems unable to separate events from their representation after the war: 'This', he comments of the German assault on Poles hiding in the sewers, 'I know from films'.[2] Events in which he had participated, albeit reluctantly, and their images in film had merged in his memory. Białoszewski's remark was not a conceit about the ubiquitous reach of the media of the kind advanced by post-modernists. It was much more closely related to the experience of living in Poland after the war. Recent history could only be represented in strained and distorted ways in the People's Republic. The particular movie that he had in mind is probably Andrzej Wajda's *Kanał* (1956), a brilliant lament for those who died during the terrible summer of 1944. Much lauded abroad and loved

17

at home, this film is a moving dramatization of events that historical accounts in the People's Republic of Poland, weighed down with ideology and contained by censorship, could relate with little candour. A taboo held public discussion of the Warsaw Uprising in check. For two months in the summer of 1944 the Red Army had waited inert on the eastern banks of the Vistula, within sight of the fighting, while 225,000 civilians died and much of the city was destroyed. After the war the liberation of the city was claimed in the official press as an unequivocal Soviet triumph, whereas in the minds of many Poles the Red Army was associated with treachery. In the 1950s Party ideologues even claimed that the insurgents ('reactionaries') were as much to blame for the destruction of the city as Hitler. In such ways the past was blurred, deformed or ignored when it could not be squared with official ideology. By contrast, films and novels like Wajda's *Kanał*, for all their poetic licence and ambiguous symbolism, provided a framework for understanding the tragedy that had befallen the country. Art could relay ideas that History could not.

Białoszewski's emphasis on the uncertainty of his memory was significant in other ways. Memory was invested with particular significance by those who opposed socialist authority in Poland and elsewhere in the Eastern Bloc. In the act of remembering lay the potential to contest the ways in which the past had been 'fixed', the myopic and crooked practice of History. Milan Kundera, the Czech writer, described this in rather lofty terms when he wrote 'the struggle of man against power is the struggle of memory against forgetting.'[3] What he had in mind were the distortions in the historical record of Eastern Bloc regimes before 1989, a year of democratic elections in Poland, the Velvet Revolution and the fall of the Berlin Wall. Memory, he suggested, could contest the blank spots and lies of the official records, by restoring those discredited figures who were once erased from photographs or by indicting those responsible for crimes that had gone unpunished. Memory could operate in a moral economy even if it often seemed to have little place in the political one.

Not all silences in recent Polish history can be understood in terms of dissent. Recall is a selective act and memories are shaped by being regularly turned over in the collective conscious or symbolized in ritual. As David Lowenthal notes, 'Far from simply holding on to previous experiences, memory helps us understand them.

Memories are not ready-made reflections of the past, but eclectic, selective reconstructions based on subsequent actions and perceptions around us.'[4] To this, one might add that forgetting is often interpreted as the suppression of that which one does not wish to recall. At the level of Polish society, the lacunae of memory have been read as signs of a troubled relationship with past events, sometimes even as guilty silences.[5] The Poles have often been accused of a kind of wilful amnesia, forgetting those Jews who had once lived in their midst (in Warsaw consistently one-third of the population from the 1880s to the 1930s). Neglect was made easier by the Nazi destruction of major public buildings associated with Jewish life in the capital, such as the synagogues (bar one, the century-old Nożyk Synagogue in Twarda Street, which was turned into a stable). But even those material traces of Jewish life that persisted after 1945 were threatened by the rush to remake the city. Long into the peace, the chief city architect in Warsaw, making the case for new roads, could report that the 5,400 tombstones in the oldest part of the Jewish Cemetery had 'no memorial value' ('nie mają pamiątkowej wartości').[6] Even more controversially, the synagogue at 31 Szeroka Street (today Jagiellońska) had been razed by the Nazis after use as a 'delousing centre'. When it was first built in the 1830s, this handsome circular temple under sycamore trees and set back from the busy road leading to the Petersburg railway station had been at the centre of religious life in this Jewish district. Repaired during the 1950s, it survived as a shell until it was destroyed again in 1961 despite international outcry.

The ways in which the city has remembered those Jews who were once its citizens has been a fraught process plagued with deep anxieties and prejudices. For some, the fact that many of the prominent Stalinists and members of the security forces during the early 1950s came from Jewish families was cause for a new kind of common anti-Semitism. Enduring whispers through thin lips about the 'Żydokomuna' ('Jewish-communist party') – an old prejudice associating Jews with Russian communism – tarnished the idealism of Polish traditions of opposition.[7] For others, it has been the absence of Jews in post-war Warsaw rather than their presence that has been troubling. In the 1980s a Yugoslav developer struggled to complete a stepped glass and steel building on what had been the site of the Great Synagogue on Tłomackie Street. It was destroyed with dynamite in May 1943, one month after the Ghetto Uprising had been

19

launched. Jürgen Stroop, the German general who fought the insurgents, claimed its destruction as a symbol of victory. The financial and practical problems that beset new development on this historic site forty years later and brought construction to a halt were interpreted as the effects of a curse – a chastisement for the low regard in which the heritage of these lost Varsovians was held and even as punishment for Polish anti-Semitism.[8]

More recently, an exaggerated 'fear' of absent Jews has been whipped up by politicians and commentators seeking to exploit worries about the restitution of property seized by the socialist state. Restitution has been a running issue in the Polish media since the early 1990s. Early on, the image of the shabby, greying aristocrat in front of a ruined manor house or country palace (usually holding a faded photograph of the building in the days of its splendour) attracted sympathy and relatively little controversy. Such buildings were patently not the 'People's' and their dilapidated condition meant that the state was keen to relinquish its responsibility for maintaining them. The dispossessed aristocrat, however, has been replaced in the 1990s by another, more vicious caricature, the 'grasping' Jew abroad. Early drafts of legislation passing through the Polish parliament sought to exclude those not resident in Poland from property restoration rights. Increasingly the force of argument, made both within Poland and by lawyers acting on behalf of dispossessed property owners abroad, compelled the government to consider compensation for those people with a claim to land or property seized by the state between 1944 and 1962 under communist nationalization decrees. Nevertheless, the politicians have continued to procrastinate (with President Kwaśniewski vetoing a bill that had passed through parliament in January 2001 offering treasury bills amounting to 50 per cent of the value of the property in settlement). They are reluctant to compensate pre-war property owners and their descendants abroad at high property values (inflated by booming economic growth through much of the 1990s) while many people scrape a living below the poverty line. Stalled legislation and the publicity-seeking actions of puffed-up nationalist politicians have meant that this matter has become an amplifier of anti-Semitic noise (perhaps most keenly heard by Poland's liberals who fear for the country's image abroad). In 1999 Sławomir Majman, a moderate writing in Warsaw's English-language newspaper, expressed a common view when he protested against the 'right of several thousand who might regain their lost fortunes [that] will cost millions of ordinary Poles loads of money'.[9] Leaders of the city's small remaining Jewish community have detected a connection between growing anti-Semitism (including a firebomb attack on Nożyk Synagogue) and the tensions caused by the prolonged restitution debate.

It would be an injustice not to acknowledge at this point, however, that many Varsovians bitterly regret the impoverishment of the city that resulted from the Holocaust and, as I will show, anti-Semitic political manipulation in the 1960s that forced the emigration of the remnants of Polish Jewry. Plans for a major Museum of Jewish History, earmarked for site already containing a number of existing memorials in the former Ghetto district were announced in 2002. The scheme promises to recreate homes, streets and entire shtetls in a symbolic attempt to represent that which can no longer be experienced in Poland except as archaeology and ersatz 'Schindler's List Tours'. Prominent architect Frank Gehry has agreed to design the building, raising hopes that such a museum would raise the city's international profile in the way achieved by Daniel Libeskind's influential Jewish Museum in Berlin and Gehry's Guggenheim Museum in Bilbao. Tourism and the city's identity are not the most important things that such a museum may enhance. Like many others, Israel Gutman, historian at Yad Vashem and prominent commentator, has argued that this building may bridge the schism between Poles and Jews: 'Real change can be brought only when we tell the truth to each other and put an end to stereotypes.'[10]

While the role of museums and monuments in rousing and sustaining, or even repressing, collective and individual memories seems clear, what of houses and streets? How might buildings and spaces come to stand for and preserve memories? After the war Warsaw, perhaps more than any other European city, was given the function of materializing memory, albeit sometimes in dubious ways. Known the world over for its almost total destruction, Warsaw's engagement with its past could never be incidental or unselfconscious. In deciding to reconstruct the city from the ocean of ruins, judgements were also made about the meanings that Warsaw's buildings and streets were to carry. Reconstruction was, as I will show in the following pages, partial and often did not encompass buildings that could not be reconciled with the new vision of socialist Poland. It also meant the destruction and clearance

Memorial on Aleje Ujazdowskie commemorating the lives of one hundred Poles executed on this spot in February 1944. The decorative metalwork includes the emblem of the Home Army.

of buildings that did not accord with the new readings of Warsaw that were sanctioned by the Party-state from the late 1940s. The building of brick walls and paving of streets might be able to represent the muscles of the socialist economy and the commitment of the city's builders, but many buildings remained ideologically ambiguous. What did the reconstruction of the Radziwiłł Palace, the eighteenth-century residence of an aristocratic family, mean in a socialist state? Such historic sites had to be narrated, explained and given new symbolic uses. Typically, monuments once embodying the affluence and tastes of the aristocracy became government ministries and trade union headquarters. Buildings and spaces alone were not sufficiently expressive for regimes that spoke through the megaphone of propaganda. Reconstruction, in the form of facsimiles of buildings that had cast shadows on Warsaw's streets before 1939, meant not only the renewal of the city but also containment of the histories that these buildings might otherwise tell.

Monuments, in their most familiar form, are self-conscious, highly visible and embodied acts of remembering. Warsaw contains more than most cities. Walk down most streets in the centre and you will come across simple plaques fixed to the walls and doorways of otherwise anonymous buildings. The addition of a stone or bronze plaque confirms the place of the site in the grand narratives of the city. A simple, even terse description of a wartime execution that took place on that spot is usually completed with the words 'Cześć ich pamięci' ('Honour to their Memory'). As if in response to this appeal, today most are still accompanied by a flickering candle or a withering spray of flowers left by an anonymous mourner. But there are other less formal and more contingent types of memorial. Inert things may be lent new meanings by association with events and people. During the war many thousands died fighting in the city, with bomb craters, gardens and cellars accommodating temporary graves until, often some months or even years later, the bodies of the dead could be reburied. For many, the city long carried personal associations with catastrophe. Białoszewski's mind, for instance, fixed on a public toilet in a right-bank park (now Paderewski Park as it had been before the Second World War) ragged by the flak that had flown during the battle to liberate the city:

> One of the greatest cauldrons it seems was right in the middle of Skaryszewski Park. After the war, no matter how many times I walked through that familiar park, particularly near the walled outhouse which was badly scarred by bullets, grenades, shell fragments, I would picture to myself how important this stupid spot was then, that history had touched it in those days, that for more than one person this outhouse was the last refuge or the last view of his life.[11]

The extent to which others shared Białoszewski's impression of this shed is unknown (and that surely is his point), nevertheless, as we will see, other ordinary places were lent common meanings, albeit ones which appear to have slipped back into a state of forgetfulness today.

If memory was lent particular significance during the socialist period, what role does it play in the shaping of the city since its collapse? What kind of mark did the political events of 1989, which journalists were so quick to describe as 'memorable', leave on the city? Capitalist modernity, so evident in the towering trade centres and global-brand hotels that have sprung up in the Polish capital at a disorientating rate in the 1990s, has often been associated with a kind of cultural amnesia. Modernity has long been characterized in terms of a volatile mix of creative and destructive forces unleashed on the world. To realize the future means to consume the past. How is the urban fabric – so strongly shaped by Soviet-style socialism – viewed in Warsaw today? What kind of traces and memories does it now carry? How is socialism remembered in the city?

Many writers have also emphasized the ubiquity and placelessness of corporate architecture. The Polish capital was, or so it was repeatedly claimed, the second largest building site in Europe (after Berlin) in the 1990s. In their global reach, the world's large corporations and the design consultants that serve them take little or no interest in the historical fabric of the cities that they occupy. It would be very easy to characterize the kind of IMF-sponsored capitalism that has flourished in Warsaw since 1989 and the wave of new buildings that it has produced as the city's effacement. What cannot be neatly reconciled in this account are the ways in which the city's fascination with reconstruction endorsed by the Communists in the 1940s, and in many ways so closely connected to their rule, appears to be revived by the post-communist city authorities in partnership with foreign businesses and the Catholic Church. This, along with the enthusiastic interest in erecting monuments to the living and the dead, including a supplicating Pope John Paul II and a reproachful Marshal Józef Piłsudski, the pre-war leader, testifies to a renewed interest in narrating the city's history. One hundred years ago, Warsaw's rival for the status of national capital, Cracow, was criticized for its *pomnikomania* (memorial-mania).[12] Today, the Polish capital, a city with a long reputation as a brash and unsentimental place, may yet attract this label.

FROM RUINS TO A CITY

One of the most striking differences between the 'popular' image of Warsaw and the experience of visiting the city today is the absence of ruins, even in their most picturesque form as a monument. Warsaw's visitors – like those travelling to Dresden or Berlin – still today carry with them images of the city in 1945, often literally on the pages of their guidebooks. For many years Warsaw has been represented as a city that rose from a barren desert of bones and dust, haunted by the shells of buildings and twisted steel. The terrible destruction was not simply a by-product of the fighting: it had been a war aim. Warsaw's fate had been laid out in 1940 in *Warschau, Die Neue Deutsche Stadt*, a chilling systematic document. Researching the city's past and plotting its future, a team of urban planners from Würzburg drew up

Postcard depicting 'Pawiak', a former Tsarist prison in ruins, 1944.

blueprints for the demolition of Warsaw and the construction of a new German burg, one-twentieth of the size of the existing city. *Warschau* would become home to 100,000 German citizens served by 80,000 Polish slaves billeted in a labour camp on the eastern side of the Vistula. The formation of the Ghetto in 1940 and the murder of the city's Jewish population was, in the first instance, a tragic phase in the Nazi's campaign to destroy the European Jewry. It was also the initial step in realizing the appalling shape of *neues Warschau*. The Ghetto Uprising of April 1943 and Warsaw Uprising of 1944 forced the Nazis to redraw their plans for the city. Responding with unrelenting violence, the Ghetto was reduced to ashes and rubble and its population murdered in a few brutal weeks: the rest of the city was put to the torch just over a year later. Hitler made his intentions plain: 'Warsaw has to be pacified, that is razed to the ground.'[13] Those civilians and soldiers who survived the conflagration were forced to evacuate. The left bank of the city must have been a chillingly empty hell in the last months of 1944, when special Vernichtungs-Kommandos (Annihilation Detachments) destroyed what remained with tanks, flame-throwers and dynamite.

Tomb of the Unknown Soldier, Piłsudski Square (formerly Victory Square), photo-graphed in 2002. This colonnade originally formed part of the Saxon Palace, an 18th-century structure remodelled in the 1830s (see illustration on page 85).

Those who visited Warsaw after liberation in January 1945 lacked suitable words to describe the devastation. In April *Life* correspon-dent John Hersey struggled to describe 'the worst urban scar in the world ... the walls enclosing nothing, the crumpled antiquities, the piles of rubble and above all the thoroughness of ruin – this Warsaw was incomprehensible.'[14] In September the English novelist Storm Jameson was more expressive, describing 'narrow lanes tracing the lines of vanished streets between the scorched shells of houses, each vomiting its dust choked torrent of rubble. With only spades and bare hands, men and a few women working headlong to clear them. The faintly sweetish stench of the bodies rotting under the rubble still clung to it.'[15]

If any city in Europe seemed likely to seize the ruin, turning it into testimony to the destruction wrecked by the war, Warsaw surely should have been it. Eighty-five per cent of the buildings in the city had been destroyed, placing it in an unenviable position at the top of a league of shattered cities. But unlike Berlin, where the Kaiser-Wilhelm-Gedächtniskirche was frozen in its broken state while the

Aerial view of Constitution Square comparing the state of its site in 1945 (left) and 1955. Such comparisons were standard fare in official representations of the city. This double-image is from the magazine *Solica* (Capital City).

streets around slowly turned into glossy shops and fashionable cafés, Warsaw's ruins were regarded as an affront, a challenge to be overcome. Today, with the exception of a few traces of the Ghetto wall (on Walicòw, Krochmalna, Sienna and Żelazna streets), only two ruins stand as monuments proper: one, a decrepit brick post that once formed the gateway to 'Pawiak', a Russian prison built in the 1830s to interrogate the Tsar's enemies; the other – more important in the ritual economy of post-war Poland – is the Tomb of the Unknown Soldier. The memorial itself is a broken section of a colonnade, the only remnant of the grand Saxon Palace that once framed the space known today as Plac Marszałka J. Piłsudskiego (Piłsudski Square). The body of an anonymous soldier who died defending Poland against Soviet Russia in 1919 had been interred there in 1925, symbolizing the sacrifice made by all Poles who had died fighting for their homeland. In 1947 it was one of the first formal memorials to be reinstated (after the authorities carefully removed the tablets etched with the names of battles in the Polish–Soviet war to avoid scandalizing Moscow). Well established in the official ceremonial

27

economy, this monument was adopted as the site of anti-Soviet rallies in the late 1970s too.

Although Warsaw's countless ruins were rarely conscripted as public memorials, they appeared with compulsive, even melancholic, regularity in the Polish media throughout the post-war period. Dozens of books and articles appeared that contrasted images of the ruined streets, shattered structures and lonely people dwarfed by the yawning desolation with the new vistas and façades being built on the same spot. The distance between then and now was carefully maintained by these visual contrasts. The ravaged state of the city in 1945 and the achievements of the reconstruction programme were, these documentary images pressed, incontestable. As the Party gained a monopoly on power in the late 1940s, the image of ruin became a central symbol in its iconographic arsenal, even more important than the figure of the proletarian worker and the red factory chimney.[16]

At first the destruction of the city seemed to present, at least to some, a kind of *tabula rasa*. Herein lay the opportunity for the construction of a new Warsaw, either on the site of the old or elsewhere. Some of the most vociferous advocates making this case in the fields of design were architects and planners schooled in modernist planning and architectural principles. In May 1945, for example, Zbigniew Dmochowski, writing in the *Biuletyn Towarzystwa Urbanistów Polskich w Zjednoczonym Królestwie* (Bulletin of Polish Town Planners in the United Kingdom), the journal of an émigré organization based in Great Britain, asked whether Warsaw, in such a state of destruction, could or should be reconstructed.[17] Witold Kłębowski, also in the *Biuletyn*, went further. He described the swelling desire to restore the historic core of the city as the 'mistakes of leaders in the name of sentiment'. Various radical proposals were produced by designers abroad for the historic core of the city, the Old Town (Stare Miasto). For example, students from the Polish School of Architecture in Liverpool proposed orderly Asplund-like modernist buildings following the traditional street plan of the Old Town and the Castle Square.[18]

The answer to the question of whether to restore or to build anew proved, in practice, to be a synthesis of both restoration projects designed to reproduce facsimiles of the pre-war urban fabric as well as new schemes to revive the city. The force driving reconstruction was a combination of pragmatism and what

The spectacle of rubble clearance in the Old Town, 1947.

Kłębowski had disparagingly called 'sentiment'. In fact, sentiment, in the form of a strongly patriotic current, as well as the changing political climate, ruled out architects' dreams of a thoroughly modernist city (one architect, Maciej Nowicki, had to wait to apply his ideas about the modern city until he worked on Chandigarh in India in 1950). The history of the reconstruction of Warsaw from the nadir of 1944 to the political 'Thaw' of October 1956 was a barometer of the changing political climate. The earliest actions were spontaneous, a word later much abused in communist jargon. People cleared the streets of mountains of rubble to make space in which to shelter and numerous small private firms offered their skills as builders or engineers. In 1945 the Społeczny Fundusz

Odbudowy Stolicy (SFOS / Civic Fund for the Reconstruction of the Capital) was launched in Silesia. It collected voluntary contributions throughout Poland to pay for building projects in the capital. Money was raised explicitly on the pretext of funding the reconstruction of contiguous districts known as the Old and New Towns and at other historic sites such as Łazienki Park. As the political climate shifted in the late 1940s SFOS secured funds for social schemes such as housing projects. And as the reconstruction of the capital moved from clearance schemes and the opening of the city's communications in the late 1940s to building proper in the 1950s, one can trace a shift towards a centralized and planned programme as different building technologies were organized by specialist agencies and the technocracy and technology of reconstruction became strongly politicized.[19] This resulted from the growing communist hegemony over all features of Polish life. What had once been contributions of time and energy freely given in the first years of peace became carefully stage-managed spectacles. Labour was organized into what were described in increasingly characteristic Cold War phraseology as 'ochotnicze bataliony' (volunteer battalions). Nevertheless, time and labour continued to be given gladly. For many living outside Warsaw, particularly the young living in the dreary countryside, these days were viewed as holidays or, more accurately, as organized and free vacations that were purposeful and patriotic. This festive atmosphere was reinforced by the entertainment organized to accompany their toils. In the late 1940s, Sundays in September were dedicated as labour days when families would work together clearing the streets of rubble to the accompaniment of musical bands. Any lingering ambiguity about the Party's 'leading role' in these actions, however, was expunged by slogans strung as banners across building sites or by photo-opportunities for spade-wielding dignitaries. The Party, rather opportunistically, sought to absorb popular sentiment into the ideological sphere of 'socialist' patriotism.[20]

Socialist patriotism might seem paradoxical in abstract or ideal terms, yet it was a pronounced feature of Party rule throughout the forty-year history of the People's Republic. When invoked, it simply meant loyal support to the state. In practice, it really described the Party's attempt to harness Polish society's traditional nationalism. The socialist project in Poland, despite tireless industriousness in its early years and the fanfares in the 1970s that announced the building of a 'Second Poland' with Western technology and loans, always lacked vision. Poland after the Second World War was not Soviet Russia after the First, despite the rhetorical claims to be 'following in Lenin's footsteps'. Ideologues rarely sought to motivate the nation with electrifying futurism or to persuade it to abandon its traditional contours, shaped by the family and tradition, in favour of the collective.[21] This was not simply a failure of ambition. 'Building socialism' in a country where this ideology had shallow footings and ordinary people had good reason to distrust the Soviet Union was not an easy task (as Stalin notoriously put it, 'like fitting a cow with a saddle'). Other strategies had to be employed. Communist power attempted to acquire the legitimacy lent by association with cultural forms that might otherwise not seem to be its 'natural' bedfellows. The past had a key role to play in this.[22] Equipped with a Marxian conception of progress, the communists claimed an inheritance from figures and ideas in Polish history. At the same time, the Party-state established a variety of social institutions and campaigns to tap national sentiment, including Służba Polsce (Service for Poland) in the 1940s, a conduit for contributions to Poland's rebirth. The remaking of the capital city was not just necessary for the resuscitation of Polish society, it was patriotic endeavour in which, in the historian Nicholas Bethell's words, the Party 'could claim the role of hero'.[23] Moreover, the particularly nostalgic form that it took was, as I will show, an attempt to maximize the returns for communist authority.

THE MAKING OF A SOCIALIST CITY

In 1949 growing controls over the rebuilding process, matched by the hardening of the political sphere, culminated in the 'Sześcioletni plan odbudowy Warszawy' (Six Year Plan for the Reconstruction of Warsaw) under President Bierut's authorship.[24] Warsaw's reconstruction was now firmly entrenched in the command structure of the planned economy. This coincided (though not by chance) with the formal adoption of Soviet Socialist Realism as the public style of architecture.[25] A core of historically correct reconstructions of buildings in the Old Town was to be complemented with new buildings following, in large part, the street-plan of the pre-war city. Some 'improvements' were also proposed. Warsaw was to become legible with long radiant vistas connecting prestigious additions to the cityscape. Centres of power like the Party headquarters were not

31

The future of Grzybowski Square as envisaged in 1949.

only to be highly visible, they were to be connected to new Soviet monuments as if fixed on a grid that would distribute ideological electricity through the city.

Bierut's 1949 plan was underscored by a kind of faith in environmental determinism, that is the notion that, in reshaping city space, new kinds of cultured citizens would be fashioned. Unlike the nineteenth-century city in which development was often chaotic and unplanned (and if arranged at all, then only by the military or imperial interests of Russia), socialist Warsaw was to be ordered. This vision of the metropolis, characteristic of the entire Eastern Bloc, has a long and rich history. It represents what James Donald has described as the 'overweening dream of Enlightenment ratio-

Warszawa Hotel in the mid-1950s.

nalism; to get the city right, and so to produce the right citizens'.[26] The capital of the future was to be a place of libraries, cultural centres, schools and theatres: 'factories of culture' that would produce a new sensibility. Architecture was to have other kinds of social effects too: Wola and Żerań, districts to the west and the north of the city, and a green belt between the centre and a pre-war housing district known as 'Industrial Żoliborz', were earmarked for industrial development. The advent of new industry in the city, particularly that close to the historic districts, was part symbol, part attempt at social engineering. If Warsaw was to become, in the words of one contemporary political slogan, 'Socjalistyczna stolica – miastem każdego obywatela, – robotnika, chłopa i pracującego inteligenta' (The socialist capital city for every citizen: worker, peasant and intellectual), factories and workshops had more than just economic significance. As Engels had specially emphasized in his introduction to the first Polish edition of *The Communist Manifesto* (1892), industry was appropriated as a social dynamo, charging the city with 'proletarian' energy.[27]

While Bierut's plan was not realized in its entirety, a large part of the city centre was planned and constructed during the late 1940s and early 1950s. Outside the historic district, with its picturesque reconstructions of pre-war palaces and merchants' houses on a tight

33

footprint of streets, the city acquired a set of wide and regular avenues framed with spare six- and eight-storey buildings. Unrelieved by detailing, many of the government offices, hotels and offices shared a uniform appearance. Set back from the road traffic, each had a double height ground floor typically dressed in stone with spartan traces of cornices, lintels and miniature porticoes. The floors above were regular, even monotonous, with small, closely positioned windows and sparse details suggesting columns and balconies. These somewhat diminished classical forms, drawn from a small corpus of buildings constructed in the city before the First World War, conformed to Soviet principles of Socialist Realism. The often-made complaint that the city lacked variety reflected not only the reigning architectural taste but also the pressing need to build quickly. It is important to stress the remarkable achievement of Warsaw's planners, architects and builders. By 1960 the population of the city in 1945 had increased sevenfold; five bridges had been built across the Vistula when not one had survived the war; 280,000 trees had been planted; and over 500,000 habitable rooms in apartments had been built. Reconstruction meant not only bricklaying, plastering and plumbing but also the clearing of 150,000 deadly mines and millions of tonnes of rubble as well as the production of great quantities of building materials by industry, itself decimated by the war.[28] A great city – albeit fragmented and imperfect – was built in a remarkably short period.

As if to vindicate the investment in the ruined capital, Party writers sought to persuade the Poles to employ a new adjective in everyday speech. 'Varsovian' was to be used to describe extraordinary achievement (as I've already noted, buildings were erected at 'warszawskie tempo' – a Varsovian tempo).[29] Each September, SFOS organized fund-raising events throughout the country under the banner of the annual Miesiąc Budowy Warszawy (Building of Warsaw Month). These spectacles, often centred on displays of physical culture and sport competitions, were designed to show the muscular youthfulness of the new state.[30] Warsaw, and the programme of reconstruction, became a kind of heroic theme organized to unify symbolically a dispersed and displaced nation living within unfamiliar borders. The dramatic adventure, as it was characterized, of remaking the capital was incorporated into the core of the Party's programme and, by extension, extended legitimacy to their authority. Warsaw presented a great opportunity for a muscular

34

The cover of *Film* illustrated with a still from the film *Przygoda na Mariensztacie* (Adventure in Mariensztat), 1952, starring Klemens Mielczarek and Lidia Korsakówna.

Cover of a 1949
brochure detailing
the construction
of the East–West
Thoroughfare.

display of the might of a command economy and state socialism as
well as encapsulating a vision of a future society. 'Warsaw', the
'bohaterskie miasto' (heroic city), became a kind of official anaphora
repeated *ad infinitum* throughout state-supported culture, whether
in numerous films such as *Przygoda na Mariensztacie* (Adventure in
Mariensztat, 1952), a romance between bricklayers, or in the press
and fine arts where writers and artists lionized Stakhanovite
workers.[31] In these representations, not only were the workers
making the city; the city was making workers of peasants.

The official celebration of Warsaw reached a climax each year in
the days leading up to 22 July, the anniversary of the announcement
of the People's Republic by the Polski Komitet Wyzwolenia
Narodowego, the Soviet creation that marked the Party's first claim
on power. On this Święto Odrodzenia (Holiday of Reconstruction),
replacing the celebration of 3 May as a national holiday observed in
the republic between the wars (see below), the state organized
grand, honorific events. From the late 1940s these took on a charac-

teristic, ritual form, central to which was a spectacular parade and the distribution of honours such as the 'Standard of Labour' to Stakhanovite workers. The composition of the marches was designed to display the unity of the nation by highlighting different social and professional groups from all over the country. Characteristically they were initiated by a 'Rally of Youth'.[32] These were far from carnivalesque festivals (although sometimes they would include lumpish caricatures of Cold War figures like Churchill or MacArthur). They were spectacles, pseudo-historic events manufactured to fill the pages of the press. (Although in the evening, the serious achievements of the day often metamorphosed into firework displays, concerts and children's parties.)

Each 22 July newly completed sections of the city were opened to the public with great pomp. The press championed the great architectural achievements that each year brought: 'Warsaw Julys – each of which brings forth a great, beautiful national gift, from which we expect joy and hope. These gifts to Warsaw come from the entire nation.'[33] All the major architectural and urban projects completed in this period were baptized by the state on this day. Many other public inaugurations were scheduled for this symbolic date in the new calendar including, for example, the new Constitution of the People's Republic in 1952. But Warsaw's new urban schemes were the most public celebrations of Poland's development. The first was the reopening of the Poniatowski Bridge in 1946. This was a 1905 structure across the Vistula, designed by Stefan Szyller. It was rebuilt eleven months after the conclusion of the war (a fact often compared to the seven years that its reconstruction took after the end of the First World War). 22 July 1949 was celebrated with the announcement of Bierut's 'Six Year Plan for the Rebuilding of Warsaw' and the opening of the East–West Thoroughfare under the Old Town. 1950 saw various schemes designed to inaugurate Warsaw's shift into becoming an industrial city, such as the Warszawskie Zakłady Przemysłu Odzieżowego (Warsaw Textile Plant Manufacturer) and the Dom Słowa Polskiego, the state printing house. In 1953 the reconstruction of the historical core of the city, the Old Town, was opened following a procession along Nowy Świat. The inauguration of the Palace of Culture and Science in the name of Joseph Stalin was the climax of the July events in 1955.

Increasingly, these schemes were, in Anders Åman's words, 'representational buildings', archetypes in the Socialist Realist urban vision as well as actual components in the reconstruction scheme.[34] In a similar fashion, each of the civic pageants that accompanied the 22 July openings was structured to render the city meaningful, to suggest interpretations for a socialist city and to forge connections between sections of the capital that had hitherto been detached and disordered, a state that Andrzej Turowski has called 'spatial anarchy'.[35] The propaganda message was unambiguous: the Poles were to be in no doubt that the ordering force at work in the capital was, of course, state socialism. Furthermore, the new Warsaw was self-consciously presented as an antidote to the pre-war city, which was usually characterized in official discourse as a fragmented, socially alienated and poverty-stricken environment under the conditions of capitalism. Party leader Bierut stressed that:

> The fragmented terrain of Warsaw before the war, divided by private business, could not offer the means of developing greater, solid foundations, nor could it summon up the prospect of a great opportunity, which is required to meet the increased, unceasing need of the great people's collective.[36]

These ceremonies also had a kind of synecdochical function. Relatively small additions to the city, sometimes no more than a matter of a few streets, they were like islands in a sea of empty plots and dangerous ruins. Amplified by publicity, their true function was to stir the imagination.

A TROJAN HORSE

How far to the Earth is it from here?
Yuri Gagarin on the viewing platform on the 30th floor of the Palace of Culture.

As the Cold War grew frostier the Warsaw schemes shifted from the utilitarian to the symbolic and the effort expended in persuading the Poles to welcome the new additions to their capital became more extravagant. The Palace of Culture and Science in the Name of Joseph Stalin is a case in point. The function of this vast building at the heart of the city was to act as a cultural centre with sporting facilities, museums, cinemas and theatres. Built on a major site (24 hectares) known as Plac Defilad (Parade Square), its construction

38

The opening ceremony for the Palace of Culture and Science in the name of Joseph Stalin, Warsaw, 1955.

entailed razing 100 houses that had survived the Nazi bombardment and the displacement of 4,000 people at a time of tremendous housing shortage.[37] Beyond its practical uses, the building had a symbolic function in its scale and as the prime site of public parades (for which a tribune was built in front of its main, eastern elevation). Indeed the authority of this building lay in its visibility and Polish advocates of Soviet architecture championed the reciprocity of sight that the building afforded all inhabitants of Warsaw.[38] Unlike most of the building work in the capital, the Palace of Culture and Science lay outside the patriotic discourse of reconstruction and, in fact, owed much to the post-war programme of high-rise building designed to change Moscow's skyline. So self-consciously belonging to the set of eight buildings that were designed to mark Moscow's eighth centenary in 1947, it was as if Warsaw's Palace of Culture and Science could offer a glimpse of the heart of empire, 'just' over the horizon. Despite the claim that the building adhered to the Socialist Realist maxim that ensured 'correct' design, 'Socialist in content and national in form', and the 'Polishness' of its architectural garb, the Palace of Culture and Science was rarely acknowledged as anything other than an imposition on the urban and architectural traditions of the city. The sources for its historicist detailing were to be found in the characteristic Renaissance architecture of the central Polish towns of Sandomierz, Cracow and Toruń. Architect Lev Rudnev and his Russian colleagues made a widely reported tour of the region while designing the building. One outcome of their studies was found in the characteristic Polish parapet, which formed a decorative crenellation on Warsaw's new Palace. For all its pseudo-Polishness, it was the building's Sovietness that mattered. One journalist wrote in 1953:

> It would be difficult to believe, looking at the Palace of Culture and Science, that it is the work of Polish architects trained and formed in the national traditions of Polish architecture. It is truly admirable, that this monumental work represents the new architectural tendencies of socialist architecture and, at the same time, forms an excellent connection to the best national traditions of Polish architecture.[39]

It has now been generally recognized that even the Polish communists did not want this 'gift' to the city conferred by Stalin himself.[40] As if to offset the violence done to the city by the imposition of this Soviet skyscraper, a campaign stressing dizzying innovation was launched to proselytize diffident Poles. The Palace of Culture and Science was almost invariably described as 'the most beautiful and most original building of socialist Warsaw'.[41] In fact, it was one of the rare examples of the repressed futurism that could still be traced in the last years of Stalinism. The building became a kind of didactic symbol of Communism's imminence. The metaphor of architectural construction was interlaced with one of social construction. A Trojan horse, it was designed by Russian architects and constructed by

Confectioner's window
displaying a model of
the Palace of Culture
and Science made from
sugar, Warsaw 1952.

Russian labour using imported materials. The 4,000 Russian workers building the Palace were encamped on the edge of the city in barracks. These brigades of young enthusiasts enjoyed, according to contemporary reports in the popular press, sport and gymnastics, amateur theatre, ballet led by instructors from the Bolshoi Theatre and the Red Army after their daily toil. The workers' camp was presented as a premonition of the future: 'The visit of our Soviet friends', reported a journalist in *Stolica*, 'strengthened our conviction that Soviet peoples should not only work hard, but should also spend free time from work in a cultured way.'[42] Furthermore, work on the building continued day and night using automated technology, a fact frequently repeated to emphasize the 'advanced' nature of Soviet civilization.

What is striking when comparing all the 22 July baptisms of the 1950s is the extraordinary propaganda campaign mounted in the long run up to the Palace's inauguration: streams of articles on the technical problems facing the engineers of such high, steel-framed buildings appeared in the papers and stories were published on its architectural progenitor, Rudnev's Moscow University (1948), which was described as the 'most beautiful university in the world'.[43] The campaign to naturalize this building into the cityscape sometimes took bizarre forms: the silhouette of the building before its construction was used as a backdrop for romantic films like the musical *Jeden*

41

dzień w Warszawie (One Day in Warsaw, 1952); a city tram was decorated with a kind of parody of the Renaissance-style parapet with balustrades that ornamented the Stalinist pile; and models of the building made of sugar were placed in confectioners' shop windows. The presumably unintended irony here cannot be left unacknowledged. The earliest and bravest critics of Socialist Realist architecture satirized its overblown and pompous aesthetic by describing it as 'decorated cake architecture' (Abram Tertz in the Soviet Union) or as 'the nightmare dream of a drunken cake-maker' (Władysław Broniewski, a long-standing Marxist poet in the People's Republic who had famously written a eulogistic 'Ode to Stalin').

Completed in 1955, two years after Stalin's death, the Palace of Culture was irrevocably connected to the Soviet leader. Not only named in his honour, the vast scale of the building stood like a colossus over the city just like Stalin's long shadow over the entire Eastern Bloc. Its ostentatious design, both inside and out, was more like a tribute to a king than a gift to the people. In an anthropomorphic metaphor playing on the near homonymy between the English word 'palace' and the Polish for 'finger', the building was dubbed 'Stalin's finger' (palec Stalina). Rather than affectionately reduce the building to a lilliputian scale, this epithet seemed to suggest Stalin's oppressive and inescapable influence at the very heart of the cityscape. Even when the building was stripped of its dedication, absences continued to mark the Generalissimo's lingering presence. One of the Socialist Realist figures symbolizing knowledge set in a niche on the western side of the building holds a book inscribed with the patrilineal line, 'Marx.Engels.Lenin.Stalin'. The fourth name was, however, chiselled out, presumably when his crimes were exposed in February 1956. Inside, the walls of the main entrance carried the name of the building in raised letters. At some time the dedication to Stalin was removed in a minor gesture of political assassination. Nevertheless, even in the 1980s it could still be read in the dusty brackets that had once supported the letters like points on a dot-to-dot puzzle.

The press, following the 'correct' interpretation of affairs in the People's Republic, claimed that the construction of this 'Pałac przyjaźni' (Palace of Friendship) triggered the 'fascination', 'socialist ardour' and 'lively interest' of ordinary citizens.[44] However, most appear to have been antagonistic to Stalin's 'gift' although, of course,

Figure symbolizing
learning holding a book
inscribed with the
names of 'Marx.Engels.
Lenin.~~Stalin~~', on the
Western elevation of the
Palace of Culture and
Science, 1955
(photographed in 1987).

there was no public expression of this view at the time of its opening. After the 'Thaw' a kind of swelling disregard characterized public opinion. Following the glut of images produced in the early 1950s, it all but disappeared in official publicity. Dominating all views of the city (without much competition from nearby high-rise buildings until the 1970s), the building was strangely invisible. It became conventional in guidebooks to stress its function as one of the seats of the Polish Academy of Sciences and home of the Museum of Technology, as well providing stages for three well-regarded theatres (Dramatyczny, Studio and Sala Prób). Its appearance – remarkable by any measure – attracted no comment at all. The Palace became a space without form. Moreover, it was widely used by the citizens of the city to exercise their everyday interests in swimming, ballet lessons, jazz concerts and movie-going. (The building has even been laced with a thread of peerel nostalgia as the stage for a Rolling Stones concert in February 1967.) The practical value of the building outweighed the kind of ideological disdain that would have resulted in a boycott. If it never became the great social transformer that it had been promised to be, it did not become the subject of rage either. As if to illustrate the point, Andrzej Wajda turned one of its stages into a strip club in his movie *Człowiek z Marmuru* (Man of Marble, 1976). A film that compares the ideological fervour of Stalinism with the growing complacency of Gierek's Poland in the 1970s, *Man of Marble* maps the memories and lives of those who had once been eager servants of the regime. A once clean-shaven and bright-eyed communist activist now runs a 'strip joint' in the plush setting of the Palace. As Wajda seems to suggest, by the mid-1970s any claims of utopianism once made both for the Palace and for the Party's vision of society seem to have shrivelled into abjection. By similar measure, the grand parade ground in front of the entrance to the building, Plac Defilad, became one of the largest car parks in Europe, a fate all the more poignant in a city where car ownership was at a much lower level than the European average.

Invisible in official discourse, the Palace of Culture slowly gained a prominent position in the counter-cultural cosmos to the extent that film critic Tadeusz Sobolewski could write, 'When I look at the Palace of Culture, I don't think Soviet gift. I think, Konwicki wrote about that.'[45] Tadeusz Konwicki, a Warsaw novelist who had used his gifts to fete the New Order in its infancy and then for many more years to criticize it, regularly employed the Palace as a spectral presence in his dissenting novels of the 1970s and '80s, often published in samizdat editions or by émigré publishers abroad. His *Mała Apokalipsa* (Minor Apocalypse), a 1979 book in which he gives free reign to his fears of living in one of Moscow's satellites, contains the following passage:

Immersed in that cloud or those few consolidated clouds was the Palace of Culture, which once, in its youth, had been the Joseph Stalin Palace of Culture and Science. That enormous, spired building has inspired fear, hatred, and magical horror. A monument to arrogance, a statue to slavery, a stone layer cake of abomination. But now it is only a large, upended barracks, corroded by fungus and mildew, an old chalet forgotten at some

central European crossroads.
A few windows wink at me like weak little flames . . .[46]

Konwicki was particularly taken with the 'magical horror' that this ever-visible building provoked among his compatriots. Its mysterious form encouraged occult readings of altitudinous rooms lit night and day when not obscured by clouds. Children addressed their Christmas letters to Santa there. Some sleepers seduced by its phallic form confessed to erotic dreams while others recounted nightmares in which they were trapped in its maze of corridors and staircases.[47]

In the early 1990s the building was exorcised by a spate of investigative articles. Journalists revealed hitherto shrouded episodes from the days of its construction. Mariusz Szczygieł wrote about the pitiless entombment of the bodies of Russian workers who had drunkenly fallen to their death in the building's foundations. Maintaining a 'warszawskie tempo' had, he claimed, been more important than the retrieval of their bodies.[48] For a short period the menacing power of this building was restored in such exposés. There was even some discussion of exorcising its ghosts by demolishing it.[49] Pragmatism prevailed, alongside a growing, although often begrudging, recognition that the Palace lent a particular and unique identity to the city that would be hard to replace. Bedecked with advertisements, the building was and remains uncertain of its place in the world. Unmistakably a socialist landmark in the city, it continues to combine its original cultural functions with new commercial ones. Coca-Cola, for instance, rents offices there. Rebranded as the Warsaw Commercial Centre in the 1990s, some have tried to exploit the kitsch value that the new business class – both from Poland and from the rest of the world – finds in the relics of socialism. A few years ago a figure of King Kong bearing the trademark of a prominent brand of margarine straddled this phallic tower turning it into the kind of whimsical spectacle loved by advertising. It appears that the Palace of Culture and Science has been transported from one class of kitsch, Soviet-style Socialist Realism, to another, neo-commercialism, without changing its countenance. The relative ease with which this reformation occurred might be interpreted as a measure of the emptiness of the building, so small had the investment been in it by the citizens of the city (though as we'll see later, even the most hallowed sites have been decked with

The Palace of Culture and Science with the clock that was installed in 2000.

crass advertising too). Neither desired nor, in a literal sense, built by them in the way that much of the rest of the capital was, it carried few emotional or personal ties. More recently the city authorities have attempted to invest the Palace with the kind of civic values that many of the liberal opponents of the communist regime argued was lacking in Polish society. They have commissioned schemes to replace the markets that occupy the surrounding park with cultural facilities like an outdoor cinema for screenings on summer evenings, when the daytime heat abates and the city takes to the streets. And at the end of the last millennium, an enormous clock attached to its spire ticked into life.[50] Self-consciously imitating London's Big Ben, an emblem of democratic authority (and perhaps reminding the city of the new, economic importance of time in capitalism), the Palace of Culture seems to be looking for a public role in the life of the city.

CIVIC MEMORY

In comparison to the Palace of Culture and Science, propaganda designed to promote the programme of reconstruction in the Old Town when it was first opened to the public in 1953 was relatively restrained and unembellished. The reproduction of images of the Old Town rested on the secure assumption that for all Poles this part of the city was unambiguously good. It was almost as if simply flashing the icon was enough to valorize the state's activities in the area. The Rynek (Market Square) and two adjacent streets (ul. Piwna and pl. Zapiecek) in the Old Town reopened on 22 July 1953. They had been painstakingly and brilliantly restored from ruins to create a near facsimile of the Gothic houses with seventeenth- and eighteenth-century façades that had stood on the site before the war. Two facts more than any other served the case for this particularly exact mode of reconstruction: firstly, this section of the city had seen some of the bloodiest fighting during the Warsaw Uprising. It had tremendous emotional appeal to those who survived the battles for the city's freedom. Secondly, the Nazi attack on the city was not just interpreted as an assault on the nation and its property, it was an attempt to efface Polish culture. Rebuilding the Old Town asserted not only the bravery of those who had fought there but the vitality of the nation.

Drawing a comparison with urban centres in the USA, Jean Baudrillard has written of the feeling produced 'when you step out of an Italian or a Dutch gallery into a city that seems the very reflection of the paintings that you have just seen, as if the city had come out of the paintings and not the other way around'.[51] In these Warsaw streets, this sensation might seem slightly less remarkable in the knowledge that eighteenth-century paintings of the cityscape by Canaletto had been employed as visual records during their reconstruction. Technically less important than the series of records made by architect Oskar Sosnowski's Warsaw Polytechnic students in the 1930s and continued by his colleagues in secret during the war, Canaletto's depictions were invoked to support the decision to remake the Old Town not as it had appeared in 1939 but as a

47

Postcard view of Castle Square before the First World War.

composite of buildings in their seventeenth- and eighteenth-century guises. Despite the much repeated and widely believed claim that, in the words of the city architect in the early 1960s, 'the Old Town now looks as it used to look long ago', what rose there in the early 1950s was very different from the pre-war city.[52] The emphasis on the earliest traceable form of the merchants' houses, convents and churches crowded into this compact district allowed conservators and architects to forget many of the awkward mongrel details and shabby outhouses that had filled courtyards and occupied the defensive walls around the district on the eve of the war. They could be characterized as 'worthless' nineteenth-century additions. Equally, historic ornaments that had long disappeared from the façades of these buildings were restored. This was, in part, a matter of taste: there was much to admire in the Baroque dress of the Old Town. However, such judgements were underscored by the kind of patriotic sensibility that the Party sought to harness. Warsaw in general, and this part of the city in particular, had hardly flourished under foreign control for much of the nineteenth century (despite the hopes raised by Napoleon's creation of the Duchy of Warsaw in 1807 and, after his fall, the formation of the Congress Kingdom, which made the city its capital from 1815 to 1830). The failure of the November and January Uprisings (1830–31 and 1863–4) ensured that Warsaw, as the cauldron of protest, was disciplined by strictures limiting urban expansion and economic and cultural life. By contrast, Warsaw before the partitions could be eulogized as the stage on which the Polish Enlightenment was made. Even during the ill-fated rule of the last king, Stanisław II Augustus, the arts and intellectual life flourished in a rapidly expanding city (with its population growing fivefold between 1760 and 1792 to 150,000 people).[53] Warsaw was improved with paving, several new avenues radiating out from impressive squares like Plac na Rozdrożu (Square at the Crossroads), new and remodelled palaces and picturesque parks, many designed by foreign architects in the fashionable English and French manner. The Castle – less improved than other parts of the city, including the old Lubomirski bathhouse, which was transformed into the sublime Łazienki Palace – became an important symbol as the site of the King's zeal for wholesale reform. Home to the Sejm (Parliament), it was here that the 1791 Constitution was announced. The first written constitution in Europe – hailed by reformers across Europe including Paine and Condorcet – promised reforms that would make power responsible to parliament and modernize the economy. Although the last king has often been represented as vain and ultimately lacking in courage, the image of an elegant and enlightened Warsaw over which he ruled at the very moment Poland's enemies were plotting its effacement has remained a potent and motivating myth, underlying reconstruction after 1945.

The decision to reconstruct the Old Town predated one-party rule and can be traced to the post-war coalition, which determined its future use as a residential district.[54] During the communist ascendancy, the standard pattern of incorporation of popular feeling through voluntary labour schemes, central planning and control, culminating in a public baptism, was orchestrated in the Old Town. When the Party took hold of the reconstruction programme there one can detect a shift to emphasize the Old Town as a kind of historic city core over any of the other functions it might have been given. Popular guides were written and tours were organized that accentuated the quarter's class history by reminding visitors that it had been inhabited by the poor and artisanal classes in the nineteenth century during the long period of the Russian partition. Frequent reference was also made to the fact that Feliks Dzierżyński, the October revolutionary, had stayed in the square in 1899 or that it had been the home of Jan Kiliński, the cobbler-turned-colonel who had led the revolt against Russia in Warsaw in

Krystyna Kozłowska and Grzegorz Wdowicki applying graffito to the Strubicz House in the Old Town Market Square, 1953.

1794. This kind of retrospective character was reinforced by the Warsaw Historical Museum, which was housed behind the façades of a terrace of eleven burgher houses flanking the northern side of the square.[55] Moreover, the buildings of the Old Town were given a kind of representational function in a literal sense. While the structures of the buildings themselves were faithful to period forms (often by using original fragments pulled from the rubble), some were dressed with new relief and graffito work by artists. These features were almost invariably historicizing decoration or vignettes designed to explain the history of the market square to the visitor and gave the place a didactic function. For example, the façades of some of the houses were decorated with whimsical representations of artisans or symbols of crafts once practised in this quarter, like Kiliński's own trade of shoemaking. Other façades were decorated with representations of legendary characters and mythical beasts, which sought to give the square a kind of enchanted quality. The top floor of the Strubicz house, for example, which dates from the early seventeenth century, was decorated with

Rycerska Street in
the mid-1930s.

graffito work illustrating the myth of the basilisk, a beast with a
fatal gaze which keeps guard over treasure, an indirect reference to
an early owner of the house, a banker. Others depicted the reconstruction itself, albeit sometimes in bizarrely antique forms (notably
proletarian putti laying bricks on the façade of one house on
Świętojańska Street). Many of the Old Town façades were treated as
surfaces onto which an inflected narrative of the city's history was
quite literally etched.

With cafés served by waitresses dressed in quaint period
costumes, the Old Town was turned into an image of a historical city
core rather than treated as a living, animated place. In fact, it reappeared as a kind of arrested, fixed place where history seemed to
have been completed. This is illustrated if one compares images in
pre-war guides with those found in publications produced after its
reopening in 1953. Tadeusz Przypkowski's photographs in *Warszawa*
(1936) depict curious, picturesque decaying streets and alleys where
a visitor might encounter the unexpected in the cracks and corners
of history overlooked.[56] It is as if in each of Przypkowski's photos

The Kołłątaj side of the Market Square in the Old Town in 1954.

there is the anticipation of an event. The photos are tenebrous and mysterious, shot at dawn or dusk. In the publications of the 1950s, on the other hand, the Old Town is an architectural masterpiece in which all life is visible, brightly lit and transparent.[57] It was invariably presented as a place where the citizens of the city stroll and gaze at the miracle of reconstruction. An atmosphere of eventlessness engulfed the Old Town in its reconstituted form. While not a monument in the sense of a venerable figure on a plinth, the Old Town took on one of its defining characteristics, that of culmination. Most monuments are attempts to end history in the sense that they mark the conclusion of a historic 'event', whether it is a life, a war or a tragedy. As I will show below, some opponents of communist rule in the 1980s sought to return History to those parts of the city like the Old Town where it seemed to have been adjourned.

AT HOME AND NOT AT HOME

There are more ghosts here than living people.
Kazimierz Brandys, *A Warsaw Diary 1979–1981* (1984)

Despite its efforts, the Old Town never became the property of the Party-state. It, and other historic simulations like the enormous monument to Chopin near Aleje Ujazdowskie (recast in 1958 after Wacław Szymanowski's original had been consumed as scrap by the German war machine in 1940), were customarily used by the Poles as places to reflect on their own relation to the city and to history. Not least, they photographed themselves in such places. Even if the mood of these photographic moments was informal, they were not casual or chance events. Everyday photography connected private life and national culture. Use of the Palace of Culture and Science as a kind of autobiographical backdrop in a similar fashion would be almost inconceivable. Moreover, the photographic appeal of these vivid facsimiles of the pre-war streets and monuments was itself not a matter of chance. All photographs inscribe an arrested moment against which the present, in terms of personal experience, can be measured. This is what the writer Roland Barthes has described as photography's 'intensity', its unerring capacity to remind the viewer of the 'vertigo of time' and 'the lacerating emphasis of the … "that-has-been"'.[58] As a kind of arrested or 'fixed' space that was difficult to distinguish from the original, the Old Town can be explored by further developing this analogy with photography.

In *Camera Lucida*, Barthes deploys two instrumental terms, the studium and the punctum, which he insists inform all acts of looking at photographs, but which can be applied in this examination of the popular culture of reconstruction in Poland. The punctum describes the searing, puncturing experience of viewing photographic representations. It is their affective capacity, a phenomenon produced in a photograph by the viewer. It might take the form, for example, of an unexpected detail that rears up from the image to trigger memory.

In contrast, the studium describes the general experience of viewing a photograph. It is a kind of 'polite' education produced by scanning details in a photograph for historical interest. While evidently not literally photographic, much of the work in the Old Town aspired to the condition of photographic verisimilitude and Barthes's terms seem to hold fast when applied to this architectural reconstruction. The state's efforts in the Old Town could only ever ensure the effect of the studium, of historical interest perhaps expressed as awe at the marvellous reconstruction. For many citizens of Warsaw, however, this brilliant facsimile possessed the unruly and subjective potential of the punctum. Despite the fact that the Old Town was a simulation, it was nevertheless one of the few places in the centre where residues of the past could be found. One Varsovian experienced the effect of the punctum when he recalled that 'the house I was born in was destroyed violently thirty-six years ago – but I can go into the bedroom I had as a boy, look out of the exact same window at the exact same house across the courtyard. There's even a lamp bracket with a curious twist in it hanging in the same place.'[59] The Old Town was one of the sites in the centre of the city where, like a reliquary, one might fancy a connection to the past before memory: this is a street that my grandmother knew as a child or here is the church in which my parents were married.

The Party's attempts to 'fix' the Old Town – just as a photographer fixes 'old light' with developing chemicals in a dark-room – were claimed as a measure of social and political achievement in the socialist present, whereas for those who could remember the city in the 1930s the experience of these recreations was often equivocal. Nostalgia is often shaded with melancholy. Warsaw could produce, in those whose lives were connected to the city, a remarkable and sometimes unwelcome sense of longing. For many residents who could remember its contours before the cataclysm, the most ordinary urban traces, even simply the name of a street, had and continues to have what Barthes might call a 'lacerating' effect. Chone Shmeruk, a professor at the Hebrew University, described his first visit to Warsaw after almost forty years in Israel. Walking with a group of students to show them the site of 12 Franciszkańska Street, his former home, Shmeruk described their journey:

I did not have to ask the way. I walked along naming all the streets, and the students checked the street signs to make sure that

I was right. I led them to Franciszkańska. There were new buildings everywhere. Only the church on the corner was still
standing. I guessed more or less where the house that I had lived
in before the war had stood.[60]

Shmeruk's ability to map Warsaw's streets recalls the classical art
of memory, the habitual walk through the city to which one attached
images. The powers of recall were exercised by the retelling of this
journey in the mind. Shmeruk does not say, but one might surmise
that he had been walking those Warsaw streets in his dreams for
many years in Israel. Even though the fabric of Franciszkańska
Street and the mould of its buildings had been entirely transformed
after the war, there Shmeruk found his punctum. Obstinate traces of
the pre-war street, the kerbstones that had once supported the gates
to his tenement, remained. On his return to the place where he had
once lived, they acted like a kind of beacon drawing his memories.

That Shmeruk was called to a place that he might once have
called home in his youth or that another writer was transported to
his childhood when catching a glimpse of a twisted lamp bracket is
telling. Both writers illustrate a particular characteristic of nostalgia,
its domestic quality. Coming from the Greek *nosos* (to return to the
land) and *algos* (sickness), it literally means homesickness. In a
pervasive sense, to be in Warsaw after the war was to be at home and
not at home at the same time. While one should not underestimate
the pride and genuine interest that the Poles took in the reconstruction of their city, for some, Warsaw restituta could produce uncanny
sensations. Reconstruction emphasized the distance between then
and now. This was a vertiginous difference that might be sometimes
understood politically ('When we were free') but seems to have
more often been measured autobiographically ('When I was
young'). The Old Town produced this sensation more than any other
part of the city. The emphasis placed on its unchangingness, in a city
that was rapidly growing around it, only added to its utopian
appeal. As Susan Stewart writes, 'The nostalgic dreams of a moment
before knowledge and self-consciousness that itself lives on only in
the self-consciousness of the nostalgic narrative.'[61] To know that the
Old Town had been remade from the ruins – as everyone does –
could emphasize feelings of absence and lack.

During the 1950s the image of Warsaw in ruins was used as an index to demonstrate achievements in the state's reconstruction programme. Incontestable in Poland at the time, the image of the ruin as exclusively a sign of the past was disingenuous. Destruction and demolition did not end in January 1945 when the German occupying forces fled the city. As a number of incensed historians have recently been keen to press, Warsaw authorities during the Bierut era (1949–56) knocked down sections of the city with inhabitable buildings to clear sites for new prestigious schemes such as the Palace of Culture and Science. Even in the 1970s, pre-war buildings – so precious in a city that had suffered such great destruction – were levelled to make way for new demonstrations of socialist progress: multi-lane highways like the Łazienkowska Thoroughfare (Trasa Łazienkowska) and international hotels. Images of ruins may have been unproblematic when used as a yardstick against which to judge the achievements of the programme of reconstruction, but their lingering presence in the city well into the 1960s was a troubling fact that was met with near silence in the media. Ruins long dominated the cityscape, providing space for illicit social practices such as black market trading, as well as decrepit homes for ordinary people. Ruins and 'delinquency', as it might have been called, seemed to fuse: prostitutes in Warsaw slang in the 1950s were known as *gruzinki* (Georgian girls), for instance, because they conducted their trade in the ruins (*gruzy*). The ruin was the setting for 'invisible' Warsaw, that is patterns of life in the city that did not accord with image of the heroic society of workers and loyal intellectuals being promoted by the Party.

Occasional glimpses of life in the ruins could, however, be caught, particularly during a short period of liberalization around 1955. Following Stalin's death in 1953, communist parties throughout the Eastern Bloc struggled to maintain their claim to be agents of progress. Although sometimes welcomed as a force for social justice with the vigour to rebuild a devastated region, Soviet-style socialism had introduced the 'cult of personality' and the terror associated with the secret police and show trials. With Stalin gone, uncertainty in the Soviet leadership and pressure for reform building, critics – both within the Party and without – grew in confidence, attacking the Stalinist stranglehold on the economy and the arts, as well as the abuse of the law. This wave gathered momentum, rocking the entire region and breaking into revolution in Hungary in October 1956. In Poland, the Party, under new leadership led by Władysław Gomułka (who caught a tow on swelling popular protest on his route to power), responded to surging criticism by encouraging a degree of pluralism and free expression. Limited criticism, like a pressure valve, would vent dissent and renew communist authority. In the second half of the 1950s, a period dubbed the 'Thaw', new forms of cultural expression like abstract painting were not only tolerated but encouraged as tangible signs of the modernization of socialism. At the same time, a new wave of 'social realist' novelists, film-makers and photographers came to prominence for their explicit criticisms of Polish life. Their gritty poems, films and novels were often set in the concrete geography of Warsaw's streets and ruins. Adam Ważyk's 'Poemat dla Dorosłych' (A Poem for Adults, 1955), a reveille sounded at the beginning of the 'Thaw', was an early example of this new representation of the city.

Ważyk was a pre-war member of the Party whose verse had decorated the Party's vision of socialist Poland. The effect of the publication of 'A Poem for Adults' in *Nowa Kultura*, the weekly organ of the Union of Polish Writers, after long altercations with the censor, was one of shock. Eschewing the ideologically distorted injunction to portray life 'not simply as "objective fact" but … in its revolutionary development', Ważyk's graphic images of poverty, emptiness and drudgery expressed everyday realities. Employing none of the conventional symbols and rhetorical formulae that had turned culture into propaganda, his poem, a dramatic cut into anaesthetized aesthetics, renewed art's capacity to object.

'A Poem for Adults' begins with a journey along the thoroughfare formerly known as Świętokrzyska (Holy Cross) but which had been subsumed into Prosta (Straight Street) after the war:

When, by error, I jumped on a wrong bus,
The people in it, as usual, were returning from work.
The bus rushed down an unknown street,
O Holy Cross Street, no longer Holy Cross,
Where are your antique shops, bookstores, students?
Where are you, the dead?
The memory of you peters out.
Then the bus stopped on a dug-up square.

Old skeleton of a four-storey house anticipated the verdict of fate.
I got off in the square in a working district,
Where gray walls become silver, reminiscing.
People were hurrying home, and I did not dare ask them the way.
In my childhood, had I not come to this house?
I returned like a man who had gone for medicine and come home
twenty years later.
My wife asked me where I'd been.
My children asked me where I'd been.
I said nothing and sweated like a mouse.
Squares turn like cobras, houses stand like peacocks,
Give me any old stone, and I'll be back in my city.
Standing, a thoughtless pillar, under the candelabrum,
I praise, admire, and curse on abra- and abracadabra.
Heroically, I venture under the splendid columns and pay no
heed to the puppets of Gallux, painted for coffins.
Here youngsters come for ice cream!
All of them are young, and yet their memories reach the ruins;
girls will soon have babies.[62]

Ważyk describes the city's new buildings – the 'thoughtless pillar', the candelabrum and the peacock house – as symbols of vanitas. The cost of these much trumpeted achievements had been great. In the series of poetic episodes contrasting rhetoric with experience that follow the lines reproduced above, the materials and images of construction form a backdrop for crime: he alludes to rape and prostitution on building sites and describes Nowa Huta, a new town near Cracow in the south, as an Eldorado being built by a drunken, lecherous mob. This was a picture of the 'bohaterskie miasto' that was shockingly frank. The vein of nostalgia running through the verses was another provocation. Alienated from the new Warsaw in which he lived, Ważyk was transported from a grey world to a silver one of his memories before the war by glimpses of destruction.

If ruins and monuments were polarized in the official scheme of reconstruction throughout the 1950s and '60s, they were not necessarily mutually inimical in the popular consciousness. Although the capacity to represent or to articulate views of the city was contained, the Party still felt the weight of popular sentiments that could hardly be declared. In the 1960s one ruin was the focus of a great deal of

Antoni Chodorowski's cartoon from 1975 commenting on the popular interest in the reconstruction of the Royal Castle. The banner reads 'The Whole Nation Builds the Castle', a play on a much-repeated slogan of the Bierut era, 'The Whole Nation Builds its Capital'.

public feeling. The Royal Castle, then only visible between the Old Town and the river as a line of foundations, a shattered gateway and broken walls, most below ground level like the site of an archaeological dig, was not forgotten. During the occupation the building was burned out by the Nazis in September 1939 and then thoroughly destroyed with the rest of the left-bank city in 1944. Recognizing the threat to this landmark, which uniquely functioned both as the seat of the monarch and as the site of meetings of Polish deputies in the Sejm, art historians during the war made covert nocturnal trips to the castle to remove furniture, paintings and architectural details. Columns were taken from the chapel and panelled doors furtively lifted off their hinges. Like cells from which a complete organism might be cloned, these details were carefully preserved in anticipation of the castle's second coming. However, Party leader Gomułka, always an uncompromising leader, is generally believed to have obstructed such plans personally. Employing a peculiarly surreal metaphor, this ascetic autocrat is reported to have said 'A cactus will grow on my hand before the Royal Castle is rebuilt.' The castle not only embodied the quasi-democratic traditions of the Polish Commonwealth, the fact that it had been burned and plundered after the Blitzkrieg of September 1939 when the Soviet Union and the Germans had formed their alliance, meant that, from the Party's perspective, the castle was a dangerous monument. Unacceptable as a symbol of regression (perhaps because it had been adopted as a *cause célèbre* among anti-communist Poles living abroad),[63] this complex of historic buildings, even as rubble, barely existed in the representational order of Polish socialism in the 1960s. Yet it occupied a prominent place in the imagined or remembered city, not least for those who made the pilgrimage to the Old Town.

Gomułka's successor in 1971, Edward Gierek, who came to power on the back of another wave of unrest, this time in the shipyards and factories on the Baltic coast, took much more care to create a stronger consensus behind his rule. Taking a leaf from a number of his predecessors, he played the patriotic card. Interested in attracting the support, financial or otherwise, of the Polonia (Poles living abroad), the rebuilding of the Royal Castle was made into a popular cause of the first order. This grand project, funded by public subscription and with donations from abroad, was announced by Gierek in January 1971, one month after coming to office. After completion thirteen years later, 'Warsaw Castle' as it was known (Royal being unacceptable in the socialist lexicon) became a showcase for grand state events and a popular tourist destination. While some of the interiors were given emphatically historical functions to represent different phases in the building's history from the fifteenth century to the eighteenth, others met ceremonial and bureaucratic needs in the present. Rebuilding was not only a shrewd attempt to tap public opinion, it checked any fantastic hopes that an empty site might nourish. In ruins, the Royal Castle could function indexically as evidence of both the glorious past and the ignominious present. Not encumbered with a purpose or function, it was open to the kind of emotional investment that Gierek later sought to contain and harness. Restored, this building belongs to that odd category of things – described as 'counter-iconoclasm' – that are remade in order to forget what their absence once signified.[64]

Dzierżyński Square photographed in the late 1950s.

HEROES AND ENEMIES

A stock criticism of city planning in the Eastern Bloc was that the patterns of diversity that had once been characteristic of Central and Eastern Europe were being effaced. Standard building types and production-line monuments were producing a characterless cityscape, particularly after the late 1950s when most Eastern Bloc states embraced modern architecture. The debased vocabulary of the socialist city, particularly on its newer fringes, included high-rise blocks, lumpy statues of Marx and his brothers, Engels and Lenin, banners with empty slogans celebrating socialist life as well as tanks on moulding plinths and deserted military cemeteries. While Warsaw was invariably claimed as a socialist city of the first order, the visitor would be hard pressed to find many orthodox monuments of this kind, even during the height of the Stalinist megalomania. Coinciding with the Thaw, the planned stone colossus in the image of Stalin, which was to stand on Plac Defilad (Parade Square), was never erected. By the time the competition designs solicited after the Soviet leader's death in 1953 were ready, Stalin's steely reputation was already shattered.[65] Moreover, relatively few sons and daughters of Polish socialism were memorialized on Warsaw's streets, although Dzierżyński, the old Bolshevik, made an early appearance as the centrepiece of Plac Bankowy, a neo-classical three-sided 'square' reconstructed in 1954 and renamed accordingly as Plac Dzierżyńskiego.

A wave of memorials appeared in the late 1960s and the 1970s as Polish socialism seemed to tire. In their latent nostalgia, memorials to the movement's heroes like Marceli Nowotko and General Karol Świerczewski – figures from the 1930s and '40s – served only to demonstrate the Party's growing lassitude. The rhetorical force of stiff jaws and unflinching gazes reserved for communist pioneers did little to draw the attention of passers-by. With the exception of the odd daub of graffiti, these bronze figures were met with indifference until the autumn of 1989 when the Poles dismantled and destroyed their local heroes. It would, however, be wrong to suggest that the citizens of Warsaw took no interest in the kinds of public memorials erected in their city or even to say that the Party-state held no regard for popular opinion. In fact, the situation was quite the reverse. When it came to matters of historical sensitivity, the Party – particularly at times when it was unsure of its authority – took care not to inflame 'public opinion'. In the case of Warsaw, the greatest controversy was attached to the role of the Home Army (Armia Krajowa / AK) during the Warsaw Uprising. The desire to salve public opinion shaped the fate of two Warsaw monuments in particular: Marian Konieczny's 'Memorial to the Heroes of Warsaw' and Jerzy Jarnuszkiewicz's *Young Insurgent*, which has stood on the edge of the Old Town since 1983.

The competition to design a public memorial to those who had fought in bloody clashes in a desperate attempt to free the city during 1944 was announced at the height of the 'Thaw' in 1956.[66] A new Party leadership under Gomułka, himself a former prisoner of the Stalinists, sought to renew its authority by claiming a new 'national path' to communism. This meant, in part, calling a truce in the 'class war' that the Party had prosecuted in the early 1950s. During the Stalinist period, membership in the ranks of the AK had been taken as sufficient evidence of anti-socialist and 'reactionary views' for the individual to be thrown out of work or imprisoned. Show trials were mounted in July and August 1951. Former AK officers were among those indicted on trumped-up charges of conspiracy. While many members of the AK had been absorbed into the Soviet-commanded Berling Army in its march westward after the failure of the Uprising, few shared its political aims. In fact, the leaders who ordered the ill-fated rising in the city had done so in the desperate hope that Warsaw would be in Polish hands by the time Soviet forces crossed the Vistula. The Uprising was, in this way, an anti-Soviet gesture as well as a furious disavowal of German rule. Despite being formally dissolved in January 1945, a few AK units fought Soviet forces for some months after. They, however, were in the great minority. While many, if not most, members of the AK had little enthusiasm for communist rule, their representation as a network of fifth columnists under orders from London was a myth propagated to justify the extension of a Soviet-type system of surveillance and control in the late 1940s.

In 1956 the new regime sought to heal some of the divisions in Polish society that had been opened by the attack on AK veterans (many still only in their twenties) in a series of public gestures that included a public memorial dedicated to the 'Heroes of Warsaw'. *Życie Warszawy* spoke for authority when it proclaimed that the monument would memorialize *all* heroes who fought and died for Warsaw irrespective of the organizations for which they fought and their political views. While this was an unmistakable gesture of reconciliation, the actual terms of the competition remained ambiguous. Entrants in what was at first an open and international competition were able to specify both the site (such was the extent of undedicated land in the city) as well as the form that the monument was to take. The open terms of the competition, at a time when the press was being reclaimed as a critical forum for discussion of the progress of socialism, encouraged great swells of public opinion. Thousands of letters were sent to newspapers suggesting not only the ideal form of the memorial (often a triumphal arch or a funeral barrow) and the most suitable site (usually one connected with fighting in the city), but offering reflection about what should be remembered. Some correspondents suggested that the memorial should invoke not only the tragic events of 1944 but the experience of the entire nation during the war including, by implication, the division of Poland by the Soviet Union and Nazi Germany. Art critic Aleksander Wojciechowski writing in *Świat* summed up the mood of the correspondents. 'This', he said, 'is not an "artistic" competition but a national plebiscite.'

In April 1958 nearly 200 remarkably diverse designs were exhibited to 100,000 visitors in Warsaw's Zachęta Gallery, including a number of highly sentimental, even kitsch proposals by amateur artists encouraged by official reification of working class culture. Other proposals were strikingly abstract, all the more so since the official conception of art had until recently been very rigid and propagandistic. A spectral scheme, for instance, took the form of a spiralling aluminium motif suggesting both a ladder and a mournful wisp of smoke. Another, one of the two winning designs and the product of a collaboration between architect Jan Bogusławski, painter Kazimierz Gąsinowski and writer Adam Mauersberger, was notable on a number of counts. It took the form of a carpet of black and red stone swelling into a barricade marked with the emblem of the insurgents strongly associated with the AK (an anchor motif combining the letters P, for Poland, and W, for 'walcząca', fighting) that had hitherto been under prohibition. The design also implied the reconstruction of the Royal Castle (or at least its façade), a building which Gomułka refused to remake.

In the course of 1958 the heated atmosphere provoked by the competition continued. Professional sculptors who felt under-represented on the jury protested to the official commission. In what has been interpreted as an attempt to maintain their privileged position, these figurative artists characterized the winning entries on display in Zachęta as too abstract and modern for popular taste. Invoking an established critique of 'elitist' modernist art, their arguments claimed to represent the *vox populi*. It remains unclear whether such arguments persuaded the official commission to announce another competition or whether other potentially embarrassing matters, such as the failure to determine the site of the monument, forced their hand. Nevertheless, in 1959 a rather more limited competition was initiated specifying that the monument be sited in Plac Teatralny, opposite Bohdan Pniewski's brutally spare reconstruction of Corazzi's neo-classical National Theatre (1825–33). While the entries were put on public display again and articles appeared in the press, public and professional discussion had less impact. The relative freedom of speech enjoyed in the aftermath of the Thaw had been curtailed by the time of the Third Party Congress in March 1959. Public opinion, though still vented, now counted for less. Moreover, the courageous role played by the AK during the war was again shrouded by a veil of silence and censorship (at least until the late 1960s when an attempt was made by groups in the Party to obtain the endorsement of AK veterans). The winning design, a

'Warsaw's Nike' sculpted by Marian Konieczny in its new location alongside Aleje Solidarności, photographed in 2002.

massive figure of a sword-wielding siren, the traditional emblem of the city, sculpted by Marian Konieczny, a young artist from Cracow who had studied at the Repin Institute in Leningrad, symbolized many things, not least the hardening mood in the Party. Conventional in its monumentalism (Konieczny proposed a figure 10 metres high on a 12-metre plinth) and bellicose in its symbolism, this design was insensitive to the acute historical injuries that the 'Memorial to the Heroes of Warsaw' had been originally proposed to heal. In fact, after being raised in 1964 (at a smaller scale than that proposed by Konieczny), as Grzesiuk-Olszewska notes, this memorial was widely known as 'Nike', a symbol of victory and retribution rather than martyrdom. The popular misreading of the monument is telling. It suggests a kind of detachment and perhaps even a kind of forgetting on the part of Varsovians. This process was compounded in the mid-1990s by the relocation of 'Warsaw's Nike' to an 'island' surrounded by roads feeding traffic under the Old Town, its original

POCZTA *Solidarność*

POLSKA 50 zł

A fund-raising 'stamp' issued by Solidarity in 1987 depicting the 'grey ranks' of young fighters and commemorating their efforts during the Warsaw Uprising.

site being required for new historic architectural facsimiles that I will discuss below, Konieczny's monumental figure stands in limbo, neither regarded in the most literal sense by those who drive pass it or theatrically toppled in 1989 like the statues commemorating the Party's heroes.

The contrast with another figure memorializing the tragic summer of 1944, Jarnuszkiewicz's *Young Insurgent*, could not be greater. Sited today near Wąski Dunaj Street on the escarpment framing the Old Town formed by the medieval walls, this diminutive figure had a long history as a kind of private monument in the setting of ordinary people's homes. Jarnuszkiewicz first sculpted the figure as a 30-centimetre-high maquette when a student in 1946. Depicting a child gripping a machine-gun and dwarfed by the adult boots on his feet and infantryman's helmet on his head, his figure was a testimony to the young AK fighters of the Warsaw Uprising. Children – many of them scouts – took full part in the 63-day Uprising and hundreds died, their innocence becoming attached to the tragedy in the popular imagination. This was an exceptional and atypical piece in Jarnuszkiewicz's oeuvre. Produced before the complex, abstract and expressive body of work for which he achieved great acclaim in the 1950s and '60s, art history has tended to regard this piece as a minor work of juvenilia. With its exaggeration of scale, this figure seems strikingly kitsch. Its sentimentality was an understandable if perhaps cloying product of a moment when the bones of the dead were still being pulled out of the rubble. Nevertheless, the *Young Insurgent* acquired a kind of unspoken popularity throughout the post-war period with many people

66

owning plaster copies. The artist himself recalled in 1994 'on summer walks I often saw, through ground floor windows, my insurgent standing with a spray of flowers and a photograph of a young man.'[67] Inadequately remembered in the public sphere, Varsovians employed this figure of the youngest AK soldier as a personal memorial. But importantly, as Jarnuszkiewicz suggests in drawing the connection between the memorial and the photograph, the figure of the *Young Insurgent* was needed to connect a personal tragic drama, perhaps the death of a brother or lover, to a common culture that found a 'moral legacy' in the Uprising. Sacrifice and courage in the face of injustice and savagery were not only inscribed in deeds during the Uprising but, as Norman Davies has noted, 'inspired the myths and poetry on which future generations could feed'.[68] Stories of defiance in August 1944, even though suppressed in the years that followed, were inspiration for small acts of resistance in the 1970s and '80s. In Jarnuszkiewicz's interpretation, the moral qualities of the Uprising were amplified by representation as a kind of archetype of innocence.

The history of this small figure took another turn in early 1980s when Warsaw scouts initiated a campaign to have a bronze model of the figure (1.4 metres high) installed on the streets of the city – an idea that Jarnuszkiewicz himself had proposed in the 1970s. Although funded by collecting waste paper for recycling and other good works, permission for the public erection could only be granted by the city authorities. This was given and the statue was unveiled in October 1983, a few months after martial law had been lifted in Poland. After the recent trauma of military rule, which had provoked violent demonstrations in most cities and seen 10,000 members of the Solidarity opposition interned, the communist leadership vainly attempted to unite society by, yet again, invoking Polish traditions of patriotism. General Jaruzelski, for instance, established PRON (Patriotyczny Ruch Ocalenia Narodowego / Patriotic Movement of National Salvation), a would-be union to rival Solidarity by representing all faces of Polish society. With most Poles boycotting official institutions, PRON's programme hardly convinced. Moreover, the justification for martial law – a case he has made repeatedly since 1989 – was that it prevented inevitable Soviet intervention, a greater evil, by crushing Solidarity. In this context, the appearance of the *Young Insurgent* in Warsaw's Old Town can only be seen as highly ambiguous: genuinely popular, it was a kind of 'concession' to the public. Yet it also had the capacity to remind Warsaw of those August days, almost forty years earlier, when Soviet troops had sat in their trenches while the city had been turned into ashes and dust.

This town's Victory Square has lost its battle: now it is only a fragment of space, closed by a high hermetic fence; some time ago people were laying flowers here, creating a cross of memory of the dead, those killed by a treacherous assassin. Now the only symbol is the dead Hotel Victoria, in front of which the tout tries quickly to get rid of his zloties, buying dollars ...
Janusz Anderman, *Poland under Black Light* (1983).

It has become a truism in studies of culture that the meanings of things are never irrevocably fixed. They are mutable, changing according to circumstance and the perspectives of differing audiences. Although culture can be policed and shaped, the meaning of things cannot, in the final instance, be imposed. Authority in the People's Republic of Poland, with its battery of censors and ideologues, never reconciled itself to this fact. From the start, the decision to salvage lost buildings and streets not only occupied the thoughts of architects, engineers and builders, it also placed demands on those responsible for the 'correct' interpretation of the past. While the reconstruction of the entire city might be incorporated into the great rhetorical project of building socialism, particular aspects of the historic city were rather less compliant. In a very literal sense, the city had to be explained and its buildings labelled to establish their 'correct' place in the grand narrative. When Krakowskie Przedmieście, the first section of the historic Royal Route (Trakt Królewski) from the Royal Castle in the Old Town to the King's residence at Wilanów, six kilometres to the south-west, was reconstructed, a number of the historical monuments were recreated. To walk along this street in the 1950s and '60s was to pass through a temple in the national pantheon as imagined in the nineteenth century. This assembly of Polish heroes fixed in bronze and stone included Cyprian Godębski's 1898 statue of Adam Mickiewicz, the poet and revolutionary, who was deified by a great cult after his death in 1855, and a neo-classical bronze statue by

Cyprian Godębski's 1898 statue of Adam Mickiewicz, photographed in the mid-1930s.

Thorvaldsen of Prince Józef Poniatowski, who died a suitably poignant, if useless, death for a national hero in 1813 as commander-in-chief of the Duchy of Warsaw fighting for Napoleon.[69] Both represented a vein in Polish culture that found glory in struggle and death for the nation. Further along this grand street, the figure of Copernicus (Mikołaj Kopernik), the Renaissance astronomer, reflecting thoughtfully on his plinth, signalled other 'national' achievements.

Krakowskie Przedmieście without these landmarks would not be the complete reconstruction that many Poles desired and, as a consequence, the Party needed. The task of the ideologues was therefore to work these historical figures into the socialist fold. Those who had lived more recently, particularly at the time of socialism's gestation in the nineteenth century, were harder to adopt than more distant figures. At a conference of the great and the good held in 1948 to celebrate the 150th anniversary of Mickiewicz's birth, leading Party figures hymned:

Adam Mickiewicz is for us a living symbol of creative thought, forever cutting through the gloom of backwardness and ignorance, and a symbol of progressive Polish thinking which will arise in the forthcoming generation to energize the revolutionary spirit in the workers ... Even though Mickiewicz was not a socialist in the scientific sense of the word as we understand it today, the pulse of history was in his heart – a passionate pulse for coming events. He was a progressive figure in the struggle for national liberation ... Mickiewicz's creativity was characterized by deep patriotism, but he was always a stranger, even in an era of degraded and false mysticism, to parochial nationalism.[70]

The romantic utopianism of Mickiewicz's political activism during the 'Springtime of The Nations' in 1848, when he formed a legion to fight against the Habsburgs, was easy to claim. By contrast, his long crusade against Russian authority had to be passed over in silence for fear of embarrassing a fraternal socialist nation. Mickiewicz's legacy – a powerful resource in a society where his verses had long been etched in the national psyche – could only be assimilated if built into the Marxist-Leninist house of history. While he may not have envisaged the coming communist utopia, Mickiewicz's actions were represented as progressive. Warsaw (a city that he never visited) provided a kind of narrative structure for this assimilation. Standing on his plinth between the historic Old Town and the new socialist city rising to the southwest, Mickiewicz was a reminder of dark days before the bright march of the working classes.

New ideal routes for visitors to the city were promoted to connect Warsaw's past with the socialist present and future. Self-consciously usurping the Trakt Królewski, a route that might have been called the 'Trakt Proletariacki' (Worker's Route) featured in guidebooks and popular films. In the 1952 romantic comedy *Przygoda na Mariensztacie*, mentioned earlier, the country-girl heroine arrives in the city as a tourist. Her route though its streets, conducted at an exhausting 'warszawskie tempo' by an animated guide, charged with the spirit of socialism, takes her from Mariensztat, a new housing district, past Mickiewicz on his plinth and Stanisław August's picturesque palace, which seems to float on the surface of the lake in Łazienki Park. Her tour ends abruptly when she seems to be lost in Constitution Square, the monumental showpiece of new Socialist Realist architecture in the city. Unperturbed, the joy of finding herself in the radiant future of socialist Warsaw is written in her smile.

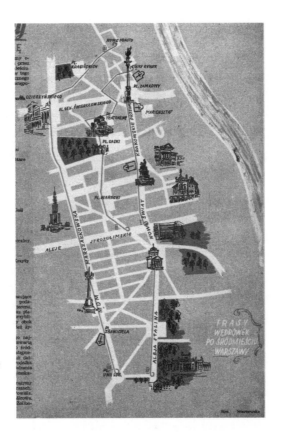

This map produced for tourists to the city in the early 1950s suggests the 'ideologically correct' route for visitors to the city.

Despite such attempts to fold the city's fabric into a story that climaxed in its triumphant occupation by workers and peasants, the deep associations of these streets, monuments and buildings remained in the collective memory. In the late 1960s, for instance, Warsaw, like many other European cities, felt the tremors of demands for reform. Students and intellectuals, encouraged by political liberalization in Czechoslovakia and agitated by tendentious reports of the Arab-Israeli conflict, challenged the Party's rule. In January 1968 a production of Adam Mickiewicz's play *Dziady* (Forefathers' Eve, 1832) at the National Theatre, reflecting on the Tsarist rule over the Poles, proved to be the catalyst that sent protesters out on to the streets. Neal Ascherson, writing in the 1980s, described this 'work about morality, religion and the nation' as being regarded by the Poles as 'a key to the present'.[71] Each night the theatre audience lent emphasis to lines in Mickiewicz's play ridiculing blockheaded bureaucrats by applauding as they were spoken.

Reportedly under pressure from the Soviet Embassy, the Warsaw Party organization demanded that the play be closed for its alleged anti-Russian sentiment. When the theatre took *Dziady* out of its repertoire, Warsaw University students laid a wreath at the base of Mickiewicz's statue in Krakowskie Przedmieście. The monument became the site of protest over the weeks that followed, during which students rallied against the system of censorship and the control of cultural and artistic activity. Some were arrested for 'rowdyism'.

These relatively minor events were exploited by a faction within the Party in an attempt to destabilize Gomułka's authority. In a grotesque campaign that led to many Poles, both prominent and ordinary, being ousted from their jobs and homes on the basis of empty accusations of 'international Zionism', and which ultimately prompted the exodus of the majority of Poland's remaining Jews, student protesters were represented as 'hooligans' and anti-socialist reactionaries orchestrated by a cabal of Jewish conspirators.[72] A student rally in the university quadrangle off Krakowskie Przedmieście in March turned into a tense confrontation when a large group of men described in the press as 'worker activists' – militia masquerading as 'loyal' workers – attacked the meeting. The trouble spilled into the nearby streets, to the doorways and churches where the protesters sought sanctuary. The police in full combat uniform cordoned off entire city blocks. This was the first of a series of clashes between students and state throughout the country in the days that followed. Accused of treachery by a Party faction that sought to revive the most xenophobic strains of Polish nationalism, the Warsaw protestors' attachment to Mickiewicz was significant. In his great epic poem *Pan Tadeusz* (1834), a work which has long had a central place in Polish schooling and established the writer's status as a 'national bard' and the central figure in the Romantic movement, Mickiewicz produced one of the most inclusive representations of the nation in the Polish literary tradition. Jankiel, a Jewish innkeeper, is the central figure in this story of a conspiracy to restore Poland's independence, set against the background of Napoleon's conflict with Russia. He is a symbol for a supranational vision of Poland that would, in Mickiewicz's words, revive 'the union and brotherhood of all races and religions that regard our motherland as their home.'[73] In making the figure of Mickiewicz (largely financed by Hipolit Wawelberg, a Jewish banker and Polish

Solidarity calendar, 1987.

patriot – not an incidental fact) the first focal point of protest in a climate of organized prejudice, the protesters refuted the impression that some in the Party had tried to stamp on them.

In such ways, this new city – made in the image of itself – could lend meaning to actions and events that might otherwise be ignored or misrepresented by the official press. While monuments were ready-made symbols, even streets could be enlisted in this way. During the first year of martial law in 1982, Solidarity supporters chose to revive the National Day on 3 May. This civic holiday had been celebrated in the Second Republic between the two world wars. Marking the declaration of the Constitution of 1791, which has usually been interpreted by Polish historians as a rebuttal of Russian authority and imperial ambition, this date had been struck from the communist calendar (and in fact from the city streets; Aleje Jerozolimskie had been known as 3 May Avenue before the Second World War). In 1982 and 1983 demonstrations

73

were mounted outside St John's Cathedral (św. Jana) in the Old Town, where allegiance to the Constitution had been sworn by deputies in the Sejm (Parliament) before carrying the Polish king shoulder-high to sing the *Te Deum* before the altar. Predictably this action was suppressed by the police with water cannons and indiscriminate arrests. The function of such memorializing events was manifold (not least to demonstrate the continued existence of Solidarity despite its prohibition) but it is important to note that the occupation of this particular street lent meaning to the event. Here a point could be made about the illegitimacy of a state that relied on the threat of Russian 'intervention' as the basis of its authority. Moreover, such demonstrations were attempts, as I have already suggested, to return History, in the sense of actions with consequence, to a place where time had been arrested in the cause of propaganda.

Although intentionally provocative, Solidarity's occupation of the Old Town belonged to an array of efforts to activate 'social memory' in the People's Republic. Although the Poles' sense of history was well grounded and the subject of frequent comment by journalists visiting the People's Republic, the politicization of history was particularly conspicuous after 1976 when attempts were made to unite workers and intellectuals into an organized opposition. A precursor of Solidarity, the Komitet Obrony Robotników (Workers' Defence Committee) was the first of a number of organizations established, in the words of one of its founders, 'to stand against terror and lawlessness, to give help to the prosecuted and to present the truth to society, countering the lies of propaganda.'[74] Organized opposition meant activity on various fronts, including the circulation of knowledge to crack the glib façade of official accounts of Poland's history, particularly of the recent past. When historical record of events like the Soviet-Polish war of 1919–20 and actions of the AK were falsified and distorted by decree, underground publishers and lecturers in the so-called Latający Uniwersytet (Flying University), a self-conscious revival of underground educational institutions during the Nazi occupation (and during Russian rule in the late nineteenth century), found a keen audience for their activities. While the police played cat and mouse with these new underground institutions, sometimes breaking up lectures in private apartments with violence and imprisoning printers and impounding their presses, it failed to stem such activities (see chapter three). One British writer reported the existence of 1,600 underground periodicals in 1985, a remarkable figure by any measure.[75]

One aspect of the opposition's work was the maintenance of a calendar of dates and events struck from the official record, creating a powerful alloy of history and memory. Sometimes accused of nostalgic, even melancholic retrospection, the opposition in the late 1970s and the 1980s invested a great deal of energy in the invention of new rituals designed to draw history to the present. To gather together to re-enact an historical event or to commemorate an anniversary was in a literal sense a way of producing an alternative society and forms of public space in the city, even if only for a matter of minutes and hours. More than just the exegesis of history, the public form of these events seemed to lend shape to social groups cast as illegitimate by the state and vindicate prohibited activities. The insistent marking of anniversaries (a practice to which the socialist authorities displayed an equal commitment) was a powerful way of bringing the past to the present and connecting events and people in the past with those who took part in these memorializing events. 'Their' identity is 'our' identity and 'their' beliefs are 'our' beliefs. Moreover, in remembering and enacting out rituals that had been performed by others before, participants acquired a sense of belonging to a larger community. In other words, the memory invested in these anniversaries was not just that of the 'original' event but of the very processes of remembrance. The stimulation of social memory, in ways I will describe below, was in all likelihood a much more collective and affective mode of representing the past than the samizdat essay.

During this period the Katyń Massacre became the critical subject of the conflict between official history and social memory. In September 1939, 15,000 Polish army officers were arrested by the Soviet authorities. Doctors, accountants and teachers, most had been reserve officers mobilized at the outbreak of war. In May 1940 they were all executed, each with his hands tied and shot with a German bullet, in the Katyń forest near Smolensk and at other places. Two years later, 4,000 bodies – the population of a Soviet 'special camp' at Kozielsk – were discovered and exhumed by German forces. The Nazi authorities claimed that these men had been 'murdered by the Bolsheviks': Moscow counter-claimed that the Polish officers had been executed by the Nazis in the winter of 1941. While the weight of evidence clearly indicted the Soviet Secret Police, this event continued to be described as a 'Nazi War Crime' until the 1980s. In 1975, for instance, the vice-chairman of the main censorship office issued a communiqué to all censors in the country allowing them to pass published references to the Katyń dead for the first time. He also reminded them of the official view, as laid down in the *Great Soviet Encyclopedia*, that the Nazis had committed the crime as part of their 'general program for the physical extermination of the Slavic nations' and that when Berlin accused the Soviets of being responsible for this massacre, it was seeking to set 'members of the anti-German coalition at loggerheads with one another'.[76] Katyń was one of the last crimes of the Stalin era to be conceded, largely because it was a stain on the pivotal Soviet myth of heroic struggle against evil during the Second World War. Until 1989 the official view of the events in Katyń was inscribed in stone in a Warsaw memorial that misleadingly dated the atrocity to 1941. Such efforts failed to deceive the Poles who adopted Katyń, not just as the site of a historic crime, but as evidence of continuing state deception.

The significance of Katyń was argued and discussed in samizdat publications printed illicitly and circulated secretly during the last twenty years of communist rule. In other places and on other occasions it was remembered more openly. Protected by their connection with the Catholic Church and long tradition, the rituals attached to All Souls Day presented such an opportunity. During this short and cold day in November, the Poles have traditionally spent time tending graves and lighting candles to produce a melancholic spectacle of faith and sentiment in cemeteries across the country. By dusk the drifting smoke and flickering light from hundreds of candles produces an ethereal atmosphere befitting the sombre mood of the day. Although All Souls had long been a public event (and had been lent 'national' significance in the nineteenth century), in the 1970s it became an increasingly political one. In the military section of Powązki, Warsaw's main cemetery, for instance, banners would be hung over war memorials asking the onlooker to respect the memory of those who died in Katyń. At the end of the day the ground would be a sea of glinting candles; red and white carnations; small pennons with the anchor motif associated with the AK; postcards of the Black Madonna of Częstochowa; crowned eagles, the emblem of historic Poland that the communists had stripped of its regal associations; and red and white ribbons. Although not an explicit description of the

Floral cross marking the spot where Pope John Paul II celebrated mass on what was then Victory Square, 1981.

events at Katyń, this temporary memorial constituted a public space where understanding of the atrocity could be shared. This was by no means an isolated event in the city. Each year on 1 August, Powązki would fill again with flowers and candles as the anniversary of the outbreak of the Warsaw Uprising was remembered. During the period of martial law floral crosses were laid on the pavement and fixed on street corners throughout the city. The most famous, on Krakowskie Przedmieście in front of the imposing neo-classical façade of St Anne's church and on Victory Square, were known as 'Crosses of Hope'. They marked the Pope's triumphant visit to Poland in 1979 when great crowds gathered to hear the pontiff say mass on the Party's own territory, a place between the Ministry of Defence and the Tomb of the Unknown Soldier. In 1979 the number of celebrants, 'self-policed' by voluntary security forces organized by the Church, made the potential of opposition clear to all. When Solidarity had been shattered by martial law two and a half years later, the crosses refused to disappear. At first cleared from the streets each night, these temporary monuments were replaced every day by the inhabitants of the city.

'Monument to the Deported and Murdered in The East' by Maksymilian Biskupski on Muranowska Street, 1995.

The stubborn reappearance of that which had been swept away might be interpreted as a minor miracle and the transfiguration of the wooden cross into fragile flowers might be read as poetry. It would, however, be wrong to attribute great significance to the temporary nature of these memorials. Not counter-memorials of the kind theorized in the 1970s in Germany and elsewhere, which drew metaphorical meaning from the slow submergence of plinths below the paving of the street or as hollow 'negative-forms' that funnel into the ground,[77] ephemerality was really a matter of contingency. When the Poles had an opportunity to memorialize their anti-communism in stone after 1989, their political representatives chose so to do. The city now has a 'Memorial to the Victims of Communist Terror 1944–56' designed by Maciej Szańkowski in the Ursynów district and a 'Monument to the Deported and Murdered in the East' (1995) by Maksymilian Biskupski on Muranowska Street, a tribute to those – Christians, Jews and Muslims – who were sent into slavery in Siberia in the nineteenth and twentieth centuries. Both have direct and literal messages that could not be fastened onto the suggestive trails of flowers and candles. Szańkowski's shrine is Warsaw's Calvary and

78

Golgotha with spent bullet cartridges driven into stone walls circling a tall cross. Each shell is stamped with the name of the site of a massacre or execution during the Stalinist terror. In contrast with the bottled pathos of Szańkowski's monument, the cemetery and street memorials, once made by ordinary people using everyday materials, directly represented a spontaneous outpouring of popular will. This was a remarkable quality that the communists mythologized but never obtained. That is not to say that these events were unstructured or even unsupported: the Church, for instance, played an important role in sustaining social memory, particularly in the 1980s when Solidarity was forced underground. The Church extended its established roles as protector of faith, distributor of charity and moral conscience by supporting culture, particularly during the boycott of state cultural institutions in the depressed months after the imposition of martial law. At the same time, Poles flocked to the churches in symbolic opposition to the authorities, as they had done in the past. The Church became a symbol of freedom for believers and non-believers, establishing itself as the only legitimate authority in the country.[78]

Church buildings became temporary exhibition spaces and meeting centres. During a dark and alienating period, the Church lent a kind of suitably melancholic and sacramental charge to the duty of social memory. Nineteenth-century literary traditions that depicted the nation as martyr and drew political messages from the liturgy were revived by artists who exhibited within the sanctuary of the Church's walls. One particularly important space during the mid-1980s was a disused and ruined church on Żytnia Street, which hosted a number of theatrical performances by banned avant-garde companies such as Teatr Ósmego Dnia (Theatre of the Eighth Day) from Poznań and works by prominent artists like Tadeusz Borowski, Jerzy Kalina and Jerzy Bereś in group exhibitions with titles like 'Znak krzyża' (The Meaning of the Cross, June 1983) and the more open-ended 'Obecność' (Presence, June 1984). The dilapidated state of this building with exposed and charred timber beams supporting a leaky roof, unrendered walls and broken columns, often lit with flickering candles, added to the conspiratorial atmosphere of these events, suggestively linking them to the cycle of insurrection and punishment that dominates Warsaw's history.

This sensation could hardly have been stronger than when, in 1984, the Theatre of the Eighth Day performed their production of

Raport z oblężonego miasta (Report from a Besieged City), based on a poem by Zbigniew Herbert.[79] As the words of this emotive and provocative poem boomed out of loudspeakers, the company's actors presented – in their trademark grotesque manner – scenes of victorious armies entering the city and public executions of those who had fought defending its streets:

> I listen to the noise of drums barbarian shrieks
> truly it is inconceivable that the City is still defending itself
> the siege has lasted a long time the enemies must take turns
> nothing unites them except for the desire of our extermination
> Goths the Tartars Swedes troops of the Emperor regiments of the
>   Transfiguration
> who can count them
> the colours of their banners change like the forest on the horizon
> from delicate bird's yellow in spring through green through red
>   to winter's black
>
> . . .
>
> now as I write these words the advocates of conciliation
> have won the upper hand over the party of inflexibles
> a normal hesitation of moods fate still hangs in the balance
>
> cemeteries grow larger the number of defenders is smaller
> yet the defence continues it will continue to the end.[80]

Available only in samizdat at this time, Herbert's 1983 poem powerfully combined his recollections as a fifteen-year-old of the annexation of Lwów (today Lviv, Ukraine) by the Soviet Union in September 1939 with accounts of the first days of martial law in Warsaw. The events of December 1981 would have still been fresh in the minds of the audience in the Żytnia Street church. Moreover, his words seemed to speak directly of Warsaw's fate at the hands of history.

Consecrating the role of memory, he wrote these lines in *Report from the Besieged City:*

> and if the City falls but a single man escapes
> he will carry the City within himself on the roads of exile
> he will be the City

This was heady and powerful stuff, invoking the nineteenth-century Romantic tradition. Yet Herbert introduced some important twentieth-century qualifications: not least that memory could become faulty under the injunction to remember:

Too old to carry arms and fight like the others –

they graciously gave me the inferior role of chronicler
I record – I don't know for whom – the history of the siege

I am supposed to be exact but I don't know when the invasion
    began
two hundred years ago in December in September perhaps
    yesterday at dawn
everyone here suffers from a loss of the sense of time

The repetitions of Poland's seemingly cyclical history made it difficult, Herbert suggested, to distinguish one's own experience of events from the ordeals mythologized in the social memory. The two-hundred-year span that strained Herbert's recall was a clutch of black dates that swirled above his head in the cyclone of history: partition and occupation in 1795 and 1939; failed uprisings against foreign rule in 1830–31, 1863–4, 1943 and 1944; assassination in the Katyń forest in 1940; and political repression by successive communist authorities in 1953, 1970, 1976 and 1981. Like a melancholic who turns over and over in his mind the events that have ruined him, Polish culture seemed locked in a cycle of repetition. The past – at least in the gloomy light of 1983 – seemed to be the present.

Although often shaded with irony, Herbert's poems almost invariably turn to matters of principle and, as such, could be accommodated in the moral high ground occupied by the Church-opposition alliance in the 1980s. Some viewed the highly reverential approach to national traditions as sanctimonious and self-indulgent, even suggesting the repression of Solidarity had been welcomed by its own leadership because it had turned them into a new generation of Polish martyrs.[81] Solidarity had made a fetish of the value of sacrifice. Something akin to this view appears to have underscored the actions of a group of young situationists from Wrocław, Pomarańczowa Alternatywa (Orange Alternative), which emerged in early 1986 and whose sardonic humour and ironic actions spread to Warsaw at the invitation of university students in the capital in the autumn of 1987. Close in spirit to the Yippies in the USA or the King Mob in London in the late 1960s, Orange Alternative are best known for a series of spectacles on the streets of Polish cities intended to demonstrate the absurdity and illegitimacy of authority. Unpredictable and loosely organized (although directed by Waldemar Maria Frydrych, a self-consciously enigmatic figure who assumed the pseudonym 'The Major'), this group made pompous rhetoric its special target. Rather than countering bankrupt ideology with reason, they often exaggerated it. Holding particular fascination for the formative years of Polish socialism, they would parade the streets chanting antiquated slogans about fighting fascism and building socialism, wearing red ties associated with the communist youth organization Związek Młodzieży Polskiej (Union of Polish Youth). One of their earliest actions imitated the rosy picture of voluntary labour painted by state ideologues in the late 1940s. Invited to join in a 'spontaneous action for the good of Polish scholarship', students cleaned the University Square on All Fools Day 1987 with toothbrushes and mops, dressed as workers from the 1950s. Singing revolutionary songs, listening to speeches delivered in the style of communist firebrands or admiring portraits of leading shock-workers was sufficient to get a number of the participants arrested by the police.[82] Later that year dozens of young men and women, well versed in the history of Soviet socialism, re-enacted the events of the October Revolution in commemoration of its seventieth anniversary. Cardboard models of the battleships *Potemkin* and *Aurora* sailed through Wrocław streets while the crowd, dressed in red, shouted 'Revolution', and a 'Komissars' Revolutionary Council' met in a pizza parlour: the Winter Palace was the local department store. Many of the participants were arrested, most singing the *Internationale* as they were taken away. Cafés and shops were not simply convenient settings for a political carnival: Orange Alternative ridiculed the regime's continued rhetorical evocation of 'the revolutionary spirit' at a time when Poland seemed to have succumbed to consumerism (a theme explored in the following chapter).

While Orange Alternative actions in Wrocław were more ambitious and comical than similar events elsewhere, Warsaw offered other possibilities. Here the streets were, as we have seen, deeply etched with meaning (for both state and opposition). Unlike Wrocław, the capital was a city where authority and opposition could be targeted even-handedly. On 7 October 1987, the annual Dzień Milicjanta (Police and Secret Service Day), Orange Alternative went onto the streets of Warsaw to 'help' the police as the official media exhorted Polish society to do, albeit in unspecific ways. Orange Alternative offered concrete assistance by directing the traffic:

> That was great. We painted our faces blue and had a big elf puppet, a drum, cymbals and stood at pedestrian crossings. When the light turned from green to red we hit the gong and when people crossed the road on the red man we pursued them and gave them an 'honorary fine card'. That's how it went until the police came and took some of us away. But we decided to fine the police so they took us all away in the end. Yes, it was very funny. The crowd applauded.[83]

The effect of this archetypal Orange manoeuvre was one of chaos. Roads became blocked with confused motorists and the police tried to arrest the amorphous group 'aiding' them. This happening also included an attempt to lay floral tributes in the shape of the letters M and O (for Milicja Obywatelska / People's Militia), mimicking the new tradition of floral crosses laid on the street at hallowed sites in the city. At the time of elections a year later, Orange Alternative filled the Old Town market square with festive 'candidates' seeking office in the Sejm. Hoisted on shoulders to deliver speeches and wave banners with exaggerated slogans and absurd declarations, Orange Alternative 'representatives' not only parodied parliamentary pantomime in the People's Republic, they also aped Solidarity's moral rhetoric and the 'tradition' of the rally on hallowed ground. To an audience schooled in the earnest discourses of the Church-opposition alliance, Orange Alternative's slogans were confusing: 'Please disband peacefully. This is an illegal gathering. Please get off the pavement. Please get off the road'. The Major expressed the surreal conditions of Polish socialism in election slogans: 'Pewex Shops for Everyone' (shops where Poles could buy western imports for dollars) and 'Exhume Stalin'. Like the generations before them who had lived under regimes of censorship and disinformation, Orange Alternative were expert decipherers of metaphor and symbol. The difference was their ironic disdain for this 'tradition'.

Today the Palace of Culture and Science no longer dominates the city skyline in the way it once did. The clutch of tall buildings that arose during the late socialist period have been joined by a rush of new corporate headquarters and speculative office developments. Glass and steel towers compete for the attention of the city and the rents of the thousands of businesses that now operate there. A building like the 40-storey Warsaw Trade Centre, designed by a Baltimore-based practice, RTKL, has been anxiously welcomed as a symbol of the social and economic changes experienced in Poland since the early 1990s. Predominantly funded by Daewoo, the collapse of this global corporation in 2000 has been accepted as a lesson in the erratic character of capitalism. The simplest narrative explaining the appearance of such buildings is usually summed up thus: capitalism is modernizing Poland both economically and materially. With the original design concept generated by international architectural practices, local architects producing the working drawings and obtaining approvals, and construction by foreign

Warsaw Trade Centre, designed by RTKL, a Baltimore-based architectural practice.

Warschau - Sächsischer Garten mit dem Zivilverwaltungsgebäude und Russischem Dom

Early twentieth-century postcard showing the Saxon Gardens with the spire of the Alexander Nevsky Orthodox church in the background.

firms specializing in the task of erecting tall buildings quickly and cheaply, they represent the globalizing forces at work in the Polish economy in a very direct way. The questions of reconstruction, ruins, monuments and memory, once so pressing, is, it would seem, likely to wither in the brave new world of capitalism. The free market sees little value in nostalgia (except, of course, as a marketing strategy). The facts, however, are not so straightforward. Since the end of communist rule a number of prominent schemes have been designed that self-consciously connect the city to its pre-socialist past, an age which was much slighted in socialist historiography as the era of capitalist decay.

As I have shown, before 1989 the reconstruction of the city's historical fabric followed the ideological interests of the Party. During the Bierut years, the restoration of the city's palaces and monuments was loudly championed whereas Gomułka's reforming and more workaday regime after 1956 placed greater emphasis on the modernization of the city's infrastructure and housing stock. With the exception of Gierek's popular 'gesture' to revive the Royal Castle, the pace of reconstruction slowed to a halt by the end of the

1970s. The desire to remake the city to its pre-war image did not necessarily end then too. Architects, planners and, importantly, the conservation lobby have continued to feel the absences and unfilled spaces, empty plots which were never assigned proper functions in the fifty years since the end of the war. Even new structures are shaped by spectral shadows cast by invisible buildings that disappeared from the cityscape almost fifty years ago. What today is the north-western corner of Piłsudski Square (formerly Victory Square / Plac Zwycięstwa), a windy and barren plain behind the National Theatre, had once been filled with aristocratic palaces and theatres, overlooked by prominent Tsarist monuments including the arching bays and tubular domes of the colossal Alexander Nevsky Orthodox church (in its belligerent scale, an architectural premonition of the Palace of Culture and Science). Restoring the footprint of the original street pattern and meeting the proportions of neighbouring buildings reconstructed after the war, Foster and Partners, the London-based architects, has designed a retail and office development for the site known as the Metropolitan Building. This five-storey, glass-walled structure due for completion in 2003 will, in the words of the architects, 'complete the missing side' of the square. The aim of replacing lifeless and empty spaces like Plac Zwycięstwa, which fulfilled little more than ceremonial uses during the socialist period (even if that category of rituals included a newly ordained Polish pope saying mass to 250,000 penitents in 1979), with the kind of compact and mixed urban pattern that once characterized the city seems a laudable aim. The continued pull of the past, however, has also encouraged much more literal-minded and sentimental developments too.

In 1997 work was completed on the former Town Hall (Pałac Jabłonowskich) on Plac Teatralny. Destroyed for the second time in 1944 (the first time in the aftermath of the 1863 Uprising against the Tsar), this building stood in ruins for ten years before the site was cleared. Although it figured in post-war discussions about how to rebuild this district (only a few hundred metres west of the historic core), official policy determined that only those buildings predating 1850 were to be remade. This was, in effect, a death warrant on some nineteenth-century structures that had survived the war relatively intact. The Kronenberg Palace (Pałac Kronenberga), a monumental structure completed in 1862 on nearby Plac Marszałka J. Piłsudskiego, was demolished a century

Reconstruction of the façade of the Jabłonowski Palace and former Town Hall, Senatorska Street. This building was completed in 1997 to a design by Janusz Matyjaszkiewicz.

later under the aegis of this 'rule'. It was not simply their relative novelty and associations with Tsarist hegemony that reduced the value of such buildings in the memorial economy of post-war Warsaw: their technical and material modernity posed problems too. As Jerzy S. Majewski and Tomasz Markiewicz have argued, politicians procrastinated over the case of the Town Hall, because they balked at the cost of the steel needed to support the open roof spans over the public spaces for which the building had been famous.[84] These chambers included the ostentatious 'Alexander' and 'Governor-General' salons, which were described as the 'most spacious and beautiful' rooms in the city when they opened in 1870.[85] The adoption of the site for Konieczny's 'Warsaw Nike' in the early 1960s (see above) seemed to put paid to any discussion about reconstruction until the end of communist rule. In 1996, however, the American financial institution Citibank funded the reconstruction of the façade of the Town Hall in the spectral image of the building as it appeared at the beginning of the twentieth century. While the arrangement of proportions, decorative details and fenestration approximate the original, the façade conceals an

87

A fragment of the uncompleted Temple of Divine Providence designed by Jakub Kubicki, 1792, photographed in 2002.

unremarkable office building housing Citibank's headquarters, ignoring the original arrangement of floors and windows. The impression of the building as the centrepiece of a Potemkin village is amplified by the memory of the extensive chambers that once occupied the first floor. Not strictly 'needed', the form of the Citibank's building can only be read as a gesture to a city whose population has been encouraged – somewhat paradoxically – by different socialist regimes and their opponents to hold Warsaw's past as a state of grace.

Business is not the only force shaping the development of the city with an interest in exploiting the powerful appeal of history. In 1999 the church authorities announced their intention to build a new church on the outskirts of the city. The Świątynia Świętej Bożej Opatrzności (Temple of Divine Providence) was not strictly a new project.[86] It was, in fact, initiated by Stanisław August more than 200 years earlier. Following the declaration of a new Constitution in 1791, which had promised to modernize parliament and rid the economy of the vestiges of feudalism, hopes had been high that a renewed, strong Poland would be able to resist the menacing intentions of her neighbours. The Temple of Divine Providence was to be a votive offering in gratitude to God for protecting the country. Work was begun on a building designed by Jakub Kubicki and footings for a massive column remain to this day in the Botanical Gardens off Aleje Ujazdowskie. Modelled into a picturesque brick monument, this martyrological symbol was employed as a meeting point by patriotic Poles during the partitions and in the Second World War. Just as Stanisław August's faith in the rescue of the nation proved to be ill-judged when Poland was consumed in the partition of 1795, a second attempt to revive the scheme was extinguished by the Second World War. The idea of offering thanks for the restoration of the nation was revived during the Second Republic (1918–39).[87] Modernist architect Bohdan Pniewski and urban planner Jan Chmielewski designed an elevated road artery flowing traffic through the centre of the city, flanked by a stepped, monumental church with a perpendicular spire. In 1938 Pniewski and Chmielewski's vision was an uncompromisingly modern statement of contemporary urban planning.

The idea surfaced yet again in the post-communist 1990s. The Warsaw Curia, in collaboration with SARP (Association of Polish Architects), announced an open competition to design the Temple of Divine Providence in the Wilanów district on the fringes of Warsaw near the end of the historic Royal Route. Although it was specified the building was to be a 'contemporary interpretation of Roman Catholic church architecture', the project itself was deeply historicist. The revival of a 200-year-old idea was to be an extravagant demonstration of the enduring place of the Church in the long cycles of Polish history. It was also a way of stamping the Church's mark on the present. With its influence on Polish society waning in the aftermath of communist rule, the building was to remind the Poles of its national role in the last two centuries. Introducing the architectural competition, the Polish Primate wrote that the building should not express 'only loyalty to a historical debt . . . but should (also) be an expression of mature faith in the principles of the Second Vatican Council, which finds Divine Providence in moral rebirth, in ecumenism, in science and culture and in the identity of the nation amongst free peoples'.[88]

After 1989 the Church – constitutionally separate from the state – made strenuous efforts to extend its influence over public and

Marek Budzyński and colleagues' design for the Temple of Divine Providence, 2000.

private life, seeking to shape new legislation on religious education and abortion as well as to influence the Polish media. Detecting signs of 'moral degeneration' brought on by the market economy, the Episcopate has taken a strong line on traditional Catholic morality.[89] Although not a product of the Church's interventions in politics, anti-Semitic rhetoric also increased significantly during the 1990s. Some of the Church's actions have done little but encourage this corrosive flow. Cardinal Józef Glemp's refusal to end the obstinate occupation of an extermination-gas store at Auschwitz by a group of Carmelite nuns until the Pope's intervention and to call for the removal of monumental crosses installed on the site by pious Catholics perhaps did most damage to the Church's reputation abroad.[90] Many commentators – both inside and outside the country – have come to view Roman Catholicism in Poland as a force incompatible with pluralism, liberty and tolerance. In light of this, the announcement of plans for the Temple of Divine Providence was not only a renewal of Stanisław August's promise to God, it was an attempt to restore the Church's reputation. The Church authorities embroidered the last Polish king's vision with new threads: this building is now commissioned to hymn the thanks of the nation for John Paul II's papacy and mark the beginning of the third Christian millennium.

In the summer of 2000 three designs were identified as joint winners of the competition with Glemp signalling his preference and casting vote for a design by the most controversial figure in

Polish architecture, Marek Budzyński. In the months that followed, the competition disintegrated into confusion with Budzyński's design coming under particular attack from conservatives in the Church and in the press. A year later a new contest among a smaller pool of invited architects was announced. The winning design was a monumental basilical structure under an elliptical dome, making unambiguous and unimaginative reference to St Peter's in Rome. Apparently resolved, the project continues to be beset with rumours of plagiarism and privilege. They will, no doubt, die away as the winning scheme by the Szymborski and Zielonka practice is built. Even though passed over, Budzyński's project warrants pause for thought not least because, as *architecture parlante*, it offers a critical and somewhat idiosyncratic comment on the uses of history by the Polish Church today.

The most striking feature of his design is a *kopiec* (mound or hill) capped with a dramatic crown suggesting a brilliant crystal eruption or, from another viewpoint, shining glass wings. The main body of the church itself is within this earth mound covered with grass and surrounded by streams, a small lake and copses. Budzyński is an architect whose buildings characteristically seek a kind of senti-mental or associative reconciliation of man with nature. (His controversial scheme for Warsaw University Library is also covered with a public roof garden and cascading waterways – see the conclu-sion.) The picturesque site for the Temple of Divine Providence is crossed with routes that pass by replicas of traditional church build-ings and through formal gardens. With its wooden temples, obelisks and classical arches, it is hard not to draw a comparison with a skansen or an arcadian garden. The *kopiec* and the routes that trans-verse the site were given an emphatically Christian reading by the Polish Primate, who saw in them reference to biblical sites like Sinai and, most obviously, Calvary, as well as to the Christian ritual of the pilgrimage. In this respect, Budzyński's design lies within a 'national' planning tradition represented by half a dozen Polish towns – including Góra Kalwaria, 25 kilometres south of the capital on the steep banks of Vistula – which were designed in Baroque imitation of the sites of the Passion. Cruciform in street plan, this New Jerusalem, first conceived in the 1670s, was the site of a river Cedron, named after the ravine between the Holy City and the Mount of Olives; a hill known as Calvary (today the site of the cemetery); and Bethlehem, a Piarist college. The Polish dimensions

Early 20th-century postcard showing Cracow's three memorial hills.

of Budzyński's scheme were further reinforced by its reference to the tradition of memorial mounds dedicated to national heroes who had fought for Poland. In Cracow, for instance, a 34-metre high *kopiec* was erected in 1820 on the edge of the city in memory of Tadeusz Kościuszko, leader of the failed national uprising of 1794. Nearby, on Sowiniec Hill, a mound memorializing Józef Piłsudski, the leading figure and dictator of the Second Republic, was constructed in the 1930s. These too became sites of pilgrimage, albeit for nationalists rather than for penitents.

While such associations might seem to lend national weight to the Church's purpose, the martyrological and national symbolism of the *kopiec* does not end there. In the Polish context, it alludes to pagan tradition too. Two further famous mounds outside Cracow, connected in the popular imagination to the historic figures of Krak and Wanda, date to the seventh century. Debate persists about whether these earthworks functioned as memorial barrows, fortifications, temples or, like Stonehenge, even as elements in a gigantic astronomical calendar. Budzyński's apparent reference to the best-known and ambiguous symbolic form of pre-Christian society introduces a note of historical disharmony that seems to check the Church's claim to be the keystone of Polish identity. Other associations are suggested by the use of this form too. Warsaw's only memorial barrow is of much more recent origin. A mound made from the rubble of the ruins of the Ghetto and dedicated to the memory of members of the Żydowska Organizacja Bojowa (Jewish Fighting Organization) who died fighting the Nazis in 1943 is located on Warsaw's Miła Street. As these examples suggest, the 'Polish' tradition of the *kopiec* extends beyond narrow limits of ethnicity and faith, the *Polak-katolik* identity in which so much has been invested, not least by the Church. Like Góra Kalwaria, which was better known as a site of Jewish pilgrimage than as a Catholic one before 1939, with visitors thronging to meet the great rebbe who lived there, Budzyński's design suggests the intertwined histories of Jewish and Polish society, and ultimately the cosmologies of Christianity and Judaism too. One should not read in his design a coded attempt to undermine the Church's authority: on the contrary, Budzyński, by his design, appears to seek the restoration of a mystical and visionary tradition that pulls the Church away from the earthly matters that have weighed it down.

YESTERDAY

The evocative power of architectural schemes with deep historical foundations seems to be growing stronger, while the city has yet to come to terms with its more recent past. The architectural conservation lobby vigilantly protects pre-war buildings for good reason. In a place that has seen so much devastation, the value of what remains is undeniable. Attempts by property developers to bypass planning regulations and clear sites of bothersome ordinary relics of the past invariably produce a rash of articles and letters to the press. By contrast, the socialist period is so completely discredited that little attention is paid to new designs constructed after 1944. Only one modern site – Constitution Square – has had much investment in its conservation, an unexpected reflection of growing antagonism to the commercialization of the city (and a theme to which I'll return in the next chapter). Unlike some parts of Europe where conservationists have turned their attention to post-war architecture, some of the remarkable structures that constituted architectural achievement and, perhaps equally importantly, were positive sites of everyday experience are now becoming new ruins. The Stadion Dziesięciolecia (Tenth Anniversary Stadium), rising above the right bank of the Vistula on a mound made from rubble removed from the city centre, designed by a group of modernist architects led by Jerzy

93

Stadion Dziesięciolecia designed by a group of Modernist architects led by Jerzy Hryniewiecki in 1954.

Hryniewiecki in 1954 and marking the dismantling of the Socialist Realist aesthetic during the Thaw in Poland, has the architectural bona fides that would compel protection elsewhere. A great open amphitheatre, the stadium reconciled the classicizing strains in Soviet architectural culture with the functional imperative of modernism. It was connected to the city in the second half of the 1950s by a trio of suburban railway stations, including Ochota and

The Stadion railway station serving the sports stadium was designed by Arseniusz Romanowicz and Piotr Szymaniak in 1956.

Powiśle, which demonstrated the floating openness that could be achieved with steel, concrete and glass. With dramatically cantilevered canopies and walls glazed with coloured tiles, these structures affected lightness as a critique of the form of monumentalism of the early 1950s. Their abstract qualities were a challenge to the didacticism and literal-minded symbolism of buildings like the Palace of Culture and Science. Moreover, as the home of the popular Festival of Youth held in 1955, the stadium carries powerful associations for many members of the post-war generation. One of a series of such festivals held throughout the Eastern Bloc, the Warsaw celebration had the good fortune to coincide with the dismantling of Stalinism. The city, decked out in colourful banners, played host to young people from the first, second and third worlds. The organizers claimed these young visitors as representatives of progress (in the words of one young British participant as 'flesh and blood evidence that in the West, too, life was developing as Marx and

The 'Europlex' cinema and shopping complex on Puławska Street stands (below) on the site of the Moscow Cinema (above).

Lenin had predicted').[91] However, to many their appeal did not lie in their political bona fides, but in the fashionable and non-western clothes and music that they brought with them. One Pole recalled, 'Warsaw changed its appearance from being a grey, post-Stalinist town to a place of lively songs that filled the streets.'[92] Today the stadium is derelict, its seating ripped out and concrete mouldering. Since the early 1990s the lip of the great bowl framing this amphitheatre has been the site of Europe's largest street market selling counterfeit goods and poisonous home-made alcohol. The Stadion Dziesięciolecia is not unique: grasping the freedoms of the Thaw, young architects designed a series of dramatic declarations about the potential of modern building engineering throughout the city. While a few of these buildings providing office and retail space in the city centre have been refurbished, many now stand rotting. They look set to become the next generation of Warsaw ruins. Others have succumbed to the bulldozer. Debate about the architectural merits of the Moscow Cinema built in the early 1950s on Puławska Street (an architectural hybrid that synthesized the monumental and axial forms favoured by Socialist Realism with the glass walls and thin supports promoted by the Modern Movement) has now become academic: it has been replaced by a mammoth multi-screen cinema and shopping mall in the North American manner. All that remains – in characteristic Warsaw style – are traces. The stone lions that once guarded the entrance to the old cinema now function as kitsch trophies in front of the new multiplex. Many Varsovians who grew up in the city from the 1950s express regret for the loss of those places that once framed their lives. The city's major newspaper dedicates much space to their voices, inviting readers to identify their favourite peerel-era neon sign or, in a strange twist that reflects the ambiguities of nostalgia for a disdained system, the 'ugliest street in the city'. Nostalgic 'sentiment' of this kind, however, has insufficient weight to resist the forces changing the city. This comes as no surprise. Warsaw, as we'll see in the next chapter, has been long familiar with economic 'realities'.

11 Shops and Markets

Where does Warsaw go shopping? In recent years, its citizen-consumers seem to be driving out to the edges of the city to shop in new hypermarkets. Enormous, windowless industrial sheds, surrounded by car parks and served by four-lane highways, have sprung up, seemingly overnight. They have become the landmarks in a strikingly disconnected cityscape of impossibly large billboards, petrol stations, car showrooms and showy new apartment buildings, much of it on private roads policed by security guards. Like mythical America, Warsaw has become a landscape of shops and cars. Afflicted with the strain of elephantiasis that appeared in reports of the construction of the Palace of Culture and Science fifty years ago, the developers of the new hypermarkets and shopping malls place tremendous emphasis on their size. Wola Park is one and a half times larger than the Galeria Mokotów, itself twice the size of the Carrefour development in Praga. The cavernous scale of these complexes is claimed to be part of their attraction to shoppers for whom a mall with bowling alleys, multiplex cinemas and theme park-style adventure games is a dreamy novelty. It seems that the figure of the wide-eyed Polish shopper, in rapture at the profusion of the consumer society, continues even today to be a staple (and self-serving) theme in reports of the economic changes in Poland. Just as in the early 1990s, when journalists would report the opening of Western fast-food outlets and advertising agencies 'after communism', political and economic change continues to be symbolized through the image of the astounded consumer.

The centripetal forces working on creating a de-urbanized landscape result, at least in part, from problems at its heart. The city centre, suffering from heavy traffic funnelled through a crumpled and old map of streets and offering relatively small, expensive and dispersed spaces for new retail and office development, is inadequate to meet the spatial appetites of these new retailers. Although the uneven nature of the city's post-war development has left windswept voids at its centre, including Piłsudski Square (formerly Victory Square / Plac Zwycięstwa) and the Foksal Quarter, the area between a traditional retailing street, Nowy Świat, and the escarpment leading down to the river, many of these potential sites are off-limits to commercial investors. The weight of history makes retail development here unacceptable, at least to the architects and politicians who take responsibility for urban planning. While history offers 'protection' to those parts of the city lined with tradition, other districts are taking on a much more disordered, even chaotic form. The thread of factories that were stitched into the city's fabric by the communists to emphasize their interest in working-class life fell into disuse when manufacturing collapsed in the early 1990s. Warsaw, like much of Poland, became a post-industrial city as the demand for the goods produced in these factories went into free-fall. As in many cities elsewhere, developers have been exploring the possibility of renewal of these rapidly decaying shells to produce new commercial space. Along Grzybowska Street, running from the new high-rise business district to the Old Town, an area popularly called 'the Wild West', shabby and cracked tenements from which the last balcony plunged to the ground decades ago and sleek, glass-skinned offices stand shoulder to shoulder. It is, however, the fringes of the city – where land is cheaper and less encumbered with history – that have seen most development. Once a relatively compact city, Warsaw has become a modern suburban sprawl.

Long aware of patterns of urban development in Britain and America, few Warsaw architects express surprise at the effects of neo-commercialism on their city. In the words of one, the capital is 'duplicating the foolish mistakes of global urban development'.[1] Architects, with their professional interests, are perhaps more critical than most. The arrival of international retailers like IKEA, Dior and Benetton, fast-food chains like Pizza Hut and Dunkin' Donuts, and monumental billboards advertising Nescafé and Coca-Cola has attracted little critical comment elsewhere. 'McDonaldization', after all, is not a concept that is likely to have a great deal of currency in a society that feels itself to have been deprived of the kinds of cultural, material and gastronomic experiences that have long been taken as 'natural' in Western Europe. In fact, the world presented by fast food retailing – the attentive politeness of its staff, brightly lit and colourful outlets offering predictable supplies of predictable

99

Auchan hypermarket on the outskirts of Warsaw, 2002.

food from a predictable menu, as well as the hedonistic imagery of its advertising – has been an attractive sign of the times. Does the lack of protest attached to the arrival of Western retailers in Warsaw, so contentious elsewhere, suggest that the city has welcomed the effects of capitalism on its body without pause or complaint? Is Warsaw being transformed from without by international businesses?

American fast-food restaurants, gigantic billboards and French hypermarkets. These ubiquitous and attention-grabbing landmarks, even in those parts of the city most saturated with socialist symbolism like Constitution Square, seem to embody the political and economic changes that have been underway since the early 1990s. Their neon brightness and synthetic colour seem to render the socialist city, already fading away, all the more grey and shabby. That Warsaw has changed is undeniable: however, the claim that the alchemy of the market has produced a wholesale transformation of either the city or the minds of the people who inhabit it is rather less certain. For many years before the collapse of communist rule Warsaw was a place – like most towns in Poland – where one could spend dollars on Western goods, both on the black market and in state shops. It had American-style self-service supermarkets in the early 1960s selling brightly packaged goods advertised on the pages of magazines. After the spartan and cultured asceticism promoted by the first generation of communist rulers, Warsaw's streets in the late 1950s adopted many of the commercial features of Western cities, such as neon advertising and enticing shop window displays. As I will argue in this chapter, the Poles were not, as it is usually claimed, first-time observers of the consumer spectacle in 1989 when journalists reported the 'drawing of the iron curtain' and the 'fall of the Wall'.

Street trading in Warsaw.

If McDonald's and other arrivals from the West have attracted little criticism, the arrival of the market – in its most literal form – has been a troubling experience shaded with ambiguity and misapprehensions. Street trading has grown explosively since the collapse of Soviet-style socialism. In the early 1990s it seemed as if the entire city had become a great bazaar as traders from Poland and the former Soviet Union set up their pitches on each street corner. New kiosks and stands appeared in the most unwelcoming places, under crumbling flyovers and spread, like a hopeful shanty town, along the city's wide Bierut-era streets. Although travelling from a different direction and selling different wares, a trader from Tashkent spreading her goods on a plastic sheet on the pavement by day and sleeping on the floor of the railway station by night represented the arrival of the free market just as much as the CEO in his suite in the Holiday Inn. In their different ways, they personify the globalizing pressures at work not only in Poland but throughout Europe.

Siren voices warn of the threat of homogenization from transnational retailing. This may well be the future, but it is not the only kind of globalized form of trade. Market trading by new arrivals to the city from throughout the so-called Second and Third Worlds – globalization 'from below' – has brought new texture and experiences to Warsaw, for too long a socially and culturally homogenous city. Cultural difference and exchange, after all, are qualities that contribute to the vitality and animation of life in the city. Markets selling 'exotic' commodities like Indian saris and Vietnamese food promise to restore lost sensations to the city. Perhaps more powerfully symbolic of the changes that have occurred here than the fast-food chains, street trading has contributed to the myth of Warsaw as a kind of frontier town, straddling a fault-line between East and West, where the market has free reign. This is a matter of some controversy. For some, street markets are a kind of embarrassing stain on the face of the city, denying Warsaw its destiny as a 'European' capital. 'Cultured' European values are posited against debased, 'Eastern' ones in what is presented as a clash of values. Others – not least the street vendors themselves – characterize this form of business as the essential and embryonic form of free enterprise. When their opportunities have been curtailed, market and street traders have even squatted in protest outside the headquarters of major corporations. As I will show, in a striking, albeit unin-

tended, echo of the past, the terms of this clash of values are sometimes remarkably similar to those used by the Stalinists during the
Cold War more than fifty years ago when they too attacked the
spread of consumerism in Poland.

CONSUMPTION UNDER ATTACK

> We loathe and detest such a kind of rowdy.
> The fancy way he's dressed.
> The mutton-head he is wearing.
> It is all in vanity's name:
> So let's put an end to his game.
> From a poster campaigning against 'hooliganism', c. 1951

In the 1950s and '60s the citizens of Warsaw were constantly
reminded of their good fate to be living in a socialist country allied
to the Soviet Union, despite the privations that they faced in
everyday life. They were perpetually on the threshold of the
promised land. Future bounty was promised in return for suppression of the appetite to consume in the present. The supply of
commonplace products was a low political priority during the late
1940s and early 1950s as the state established the means to regulate
and shape consumption. This took the form of control over
retailing by eliminating private shops as well as prohibition of
certain goods. This was initially known as the 'bitwa o handel'
(battle over trade), which was waged from the spring of 1947
before the communists assumed full power.[2] Although denuncia-
tions of 'profiteers, speculators and dishonest merchants' were
largely expressed with the aim of controlling prices of essential
commodities, like food for a hungry population, some particularly
'anty społeczne' (anti-social) commodities such as western music
or motorcars were singled out. In Poland, however, provision of
basic consumer goods was a matter of urgency. Levels of destruction
in many cities – not just Warsaw – were extremely high and, consequently, the need for everyday goods like furniture and utensils
was very strong. Not surprisingly, luxury was ruled unacceptable
by the sober mood that accompanied the period of reconstruction
as well as by the Party's inflated attack on the excesses and luxuries of bourgeois life. The moral economy that operated during the
period of reconstruction meant that popular opinion disapproved

of conspicuous consumption (without necessarily affirming the Party's vilification of the private shopkeeper and other visible members of the 'bourgeoisie').

Restraint was more than just a matter of hard-nosed austerity measures (after all, rationing was a feature of the mixed economies of Western Europe at this time as well). Consumption, in the context of the Cold War, became a symbolic field of conflict on which allies and enemies could be plotted. For instance, a campaign was mounted against the Bikiniarze (Bikini Boys), young people largely from Warsaw who affected, as devotees of American popular culture, 'nietowarzyski' and distinctly 'niepartyjny' (unpartylike) styles of dress and mannerisms.[3] The Bikiniarze engaged in a form of highly conspicuous consumption, dressing and living out what they imagined to be the style of fashionable American youth: their preferred music was jazz; their cigarettes were Camels; they adopted English nicknames from American movies and popular songs. During the height of Stalinism in Poland, the state stigmatized the Bikiniarze by characterizing them as 'chuligani' (hooligans) engaged in anti-social, promiscuous and immoral behaviour. Like many contemporary reports of spectacular youth cultures in the West, this characterization placed stress on an 'unprincipled' desire to consume. Moreover, it tended to focus on the Bikiniarze's obsessive interest in the details of a disparaged material culture, that of the USA. In October 1947, following Andrei Zhdanov's lead in the Soviet Union, the Central Committee launched a campaign in the press and schools against the 'American way of life' and its influence in Poland. The 'American way of life' – a caricature – was associated with the impoverishment and commercialization of culture. Adam Ważyk, in his poem *Piosenka o Coca-cola*, described the drink as 'the official symbol of the horrors of American civilization'. Similarly, 'Americanization' was introduced into the Polish vocabulary with negative associations, particularly when describing the effects of the Marshall Aid programme in Western Europe. Leopold Tyrmand describes how an exhibition entitled *Oto Ameryka* (This is America), which circulated through the people's republics in early 1952, sought to ridicule 'capitalist culture' by exhibiting kitsch.[4] The USA could be understood by the banal things that Americans reputedly consumed, not least debased 'Brother Karamazov comic books'. Despite the best efforts of the authorities, this exhibition proved to be extremely popular not least, one might reasonably assume, with the Bikiniarze. According

Publicity from an anti-hooligan campaign of the early 1950s identifying the profligate consumption of clothes, alcohol and 'Camel' cigarettes.

to one author, 'People wanted to see something American – to look, if only for a moment at something made across the Ocean . . . This was an unhappy love, a totally unrequited love.'[5]

At the same time 'private life' was a condition also viewed with suspicion by the Stalinists. In 1950, for example, a 'discussion' held in the pages of *Sztandar Młodych* (Banner of Youth), the organ of the Związek Młodzieży Polskiej (ZMP / Union of Polish Youth), rehearsed the most fervent position of those who supported the right of the Party organization to shape all aspects of life. This was prompted by a non-conformist letter from Comrade Jankowska, which claimed that, besides 'work in school or factory . . . discussions on the subject of Marx and the People's Republic of China and studying Stalin', even the most ardent activist should be able to enjoy 'non-controlled' pleasures such as using make-up or be able 'to dance with a comrade in suede boots . . .'. According to the results of a questionnaire conducted by the paper's editors, it was widely and enthusiastically agreed that the private lives of communist youth should be 'completely subordinated to the interests of class warfare' and that to demand 'non-controlled' pleasures was to display signs of 'bourgeois individualism'.[6] The essentially public and ascetic culture promoted by the most zealous strains of Polish Stalinism viewed the feminine and private values that might be expressed in the consumption of commonplace things – even domesticity itself – with suspicion. As Ivan Berend has noted 'Forced collectivism . . . embodied peevish intolerance against otherness.'[7]

In a polarization characteristic of Soviet ideology since the 1920s, 'profligate' consumption was contrasted against worthy production. In fact, a hierarchy of virtue credited those fields of production most distant from domestic consumption with greatest social worth: engineering, mining and steel production were adopted as symbols of the vigour of communist industry. These sectors were personified in the celebrity accorded to labour heroes such as Wincenty Pstrowski, a miner credited with great feats of productivity.[8] Reports of their achievements often contained altruistic expressions of the satisfaction to be found in deferring consumption: 'After all, we do not work with the immediate aim of consuming. Today we lay the greatest stress on the manufacture of those products that will further our industry.'[9] In 1950 Wojciech Fangor painted *Postacie* (Figures), an archetypal expression of the Stalinist exaltation of production over consumption. Three figures are shown standing in front of the kind of Socialist Realist building being planned for Warsaw at that time. Two are dressed in the stereotypical uniform of the worker, their productivity symbolized in the firm grasp of a pickaxe or shovel: the third figure, heavily made-up and clothed in a fashionably cut dress printed with the words 'Coca-Cola' and 'Wall Street', clutches on to her purse, a sign of selfish desires. The steady gaze of labour casts an accusation at this extravagant figure who hides behind dark sunglasses. Fangor's painting reproduced a cluster of binary oppositions that were conjoined in communist ideology in the early 1950s: production/consumption; work/leisure; masculine/feminine and Soviet/West.

Exceptions to the negative characterization of consumption did exist. The worker employed in nationalized factories and reconstruction schemes was encouraged to beat production targets with material rewards. From 1948 mass labour competitions were initiated with bonuses or prizes (usually radios and sewing machines)

Postacie (Figures), oil painting by Wojciech Fangor, 1950.

being awarded to the winners. The relatively luxurious and scarce goods offered as reward for hard work in 'the path of building socialism' escaped the bad odour of commodification because they were awarded by the state to the worker. They were a public demonstration of the productivity of the socialist economy. The gift – whether from state to citizens or from one fraternal people to another – was a highly ritualized feature of socialist life. During the reconstruction years, great propaganda was made of the 'gifts' of raw materials from quarries around the country (the granite to remake Zygmunt's Column in Plac Zamkowy (Castle Square), an icon of reconstruction, was given with great ceremony by a Silesian quarry, which had until recently been part of Germany and was, as such, a new symbol of national unity) and urban 'hardware' like trams and radio transmitters, which were 'given' by the workers of the Soviet Union. The most prominent of all these 'gifts of friendship' was, of course, the Palace of Culture and Science. The symbolism of the gift can also be traced in the rhapsodic promotion of spontaneity and volunteerism. Workers 'gave' part of their wages to fund construction of the new party

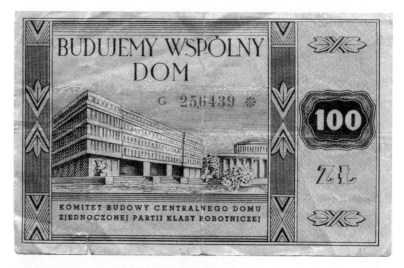

A share issued in 1949 in exchange for contributions deducted from wages used to pay for the construction of the Dom Partii (Party Headquarters) on the corner of Nowy Świat and Aleje Jerozolimskie.

headquarters, a tithe they had little choice but to accept. The characterization of labour, materials and equipment as altruistic gestures suggested the triumph of new values and the eschewal of profit. However, most recognized that these 'gifts' came at a price. With the suppression of the free market, consumption was clearly determined by politics. The Poles quickly came to realize that the distribution and availability of almost all products was in the gift of the state.

In 1954 the journalist Leopold Tyrmand kept a diary of his life in Warsaw. An eclectic set of reflections on popular culture as well as literature, and sardonic comments about the communist regime, *Dziennik 1954*, contained some reflections on the 'communist style of life'. Tyrmand, for example, recorded on 5 March that:

In Warsaw you can feel the heated preparations for the second PZPR (Polish United Workers Party) congress. It will be a weighty political event in Polish life. At once goods appear in great profusion, as if thrown into the shops. It is always this way. Great assemblies, congresses, national and international conferences result in shop displays garnished with expensive commodities. You can now acquire without difficulty sausage, sprats and better material for trousers . . . I overheard a lovely conversation on the

108

bus today. An old, fat woman – the kind who is mistress of the house – said, 'You know, beef sirloin can be had at our co-operative shop . . .'. The old thin woman – the kind who is a professional clerk – replied 'Of course, it's the congress . . .'.[10]

If sporadic abundance in the shops – described by one cynical observer well versed in Russian history as 'Potemkin prosperity' – could be understood as being politically managed, so, of course, could routine shortage.

SHOPPING WITH STALIN

. . . there is something . . . in Nowy Świat and the other streets of Warsaw which gives the city an air of drabness – the uniformity of its shop windows, and the total absence of publicity and neon lights. There is nothing to strike the eye, nothing to surprise. One almost has to put one's nose inside each shop to find out whether it is a grocer's or a barber's. Even the cinemas and the theatres seem to have done their best to hide themselves.[11]
K. S. Karol, September 1957

In the first years after the war, as the communists sought to consolidate their authority over Poland, a mixed economy first came under the discipline of the Three-Year Plan (1947–9), and then was brought under total control by a programme of nationalization guided by the Six-Year Plan passed by parliament in July 1950. Consequently, between 1947 and 1955 the number of private retailers in Poland dropped dramatically to a fraction of the 1947 figure (little more than 5 per cent).[12] In tandem with campaigns against the black market and speculation, the range and disposition of shops throughout the country came under centralized control. Planners established norms so that each locality would be served by a predetermined number of shops selling a specified range of products. 'Społem', a co-operative business established in 1908 and effectively nationalized in 1948, for example, sold basic foodstuffs in the towns, while 'Delikatesy', a new feature in the urban landscape from 1952, sold more luxurious items such as imported goods like coffee, confectionery and Russian Champagne. Clothes and consumer durables, when available, were sold in central department stores, known as a 'Pedet' (Powszechny Dom Towarowy), found in many towns and cities. By establishing a certain hierarchy of functions and more generally by keeping consumption under tight rein, competition between shops was largely extinguished.

The nationalization of retailing in the early 1950s had effects in other aspects of Polish life. Advertisements – unnecessary in a command economy and, by this time, taken as a symptom of the malaise of capitalism – rapidly disappeared from the pages of Polish magazines and from city streets. In fact, Polish commentators such as Ignacy Witz, a painter and critic, writing in *Życie Warszawy* in 1953, drew a comparison between the political and cultural posters celebrating May Day or announcing the latest film in Polish cinemas and commercial advertising in the West:

> Capitalist advertising posters do not convince, do not speak, do not teach: they simply scream. Our poster is a professional friend of the masses . . . The difference between posters of capitalist societies and those in progressive countries is like that between a lying, noisy trader and a cultured, whole-hearted advocate of the rights of society.[13]

For Witz the clamorousness of the street in the West was measure of the 'decadence' of the system that shaped it.

The widely used propaganda technique of binary opposition – in Witz's case between West and East – was also employed to draw comparison between present conditions and life before the Second World War. *Stolica*, a weekly magazine dedicated to the reconstruction of Warsaw, often reproduced contrasting pictures of Warsaw past and present. In a typical observation, the classical Bentkowski House dating from the Congress Kingdom on Nowy Świat, once a major commercial street in the capital, was revealed in a 1939 image as once having been disfigured with 'tempting' signs and advertisements for the 'business interests' that occupied its ground floors. This photograph, contrasted with another demonstrating its unpolluted state and new role as a scientific institute in 1953, was presented as a measure of the new value system prevailing in Poland.[14]

The Bentkowski house on Nowy Świat photographed before and after the Second
World War to demonstrate the building's 'improvement' in socialist conditions.

The Stalinist assault on commerce drew upon a deeply embedded vein in national mythology, that of the pre-eminence of culture.[15] To be 'kulturalny' (cultured) has been a confidently asserted state of being since the early nineteenth century (in fact since the legal dissolution of the *szlachta*, the nobility, in 1795 by the partitioning powers).[16] This, of course, has been a general European phenomenon but the particular circumstances of Polish history gave added emphasis to the 'value' of culture. Hampered by strictures placed on public life during the period of partitions (1795–1918) as well as by the under-development of a commercial, bourgeois class, some Poles postulated an ideal Polishness based on high levels of education and a traditional notion of social and moral conduct. These two qualities were connected in that one should be knowledgeable about culture in order to draw from it lessons for the conduct of life, of whatever station (although the pull of the *kultura szlachecka*, noble ethos, was always 'up' the social scale). In the 1950s the communists, despite their pretensions to be the vanguard of the working class, sustained this idealistic though inherently elitist view of culture as an edifying force (conveniently echoing Lenin, who had argued after 1917 that it was necessary to hold on to the finest aspects of Russian culture to build a more cultured society).[17] 'Kulturalny' attitudes and patterns of consumption were heavily promoted in state propaganda: ordinary Poles were invited – particularly during the Dni oświaty, książki i prasy (Days of education, literature and the press), a campaign mounted each May – to purchase 'improving' cultural products such as nineteenth-century novels and Russian language publications. By the same measure, failure to maintain 'kulturalny' patterns of behaviour was cast as anti-social. Poles were reminded, for example, that 'a cultured person does not get drunk' in campaigns against alcoholism by the social affairs section of WAG, the state publishing house.

Culture and commerce were generally polarized in the discourse over consumption. An echo of the disdain in which commerce was held can be found in 1954 when *Świat*, a photojournal based on *Life* magazine, reproduced a touched-up photograph of an Italian highway marred by a rash of advertisements for petrol.[18] In the accompanying article entitled 'Zamerykanizowany krajobraz' (Americanized landscape), the author elaborated a comparison

MDM cigarette
packaging, early 1950s.

between the beautiful landscape (nature improved by culture) and
the trickery of advertising (culture spoiled by greed). Advertising
was an index of the corruption of culture. The benefits of culture,
however, could be brought to salvage the defects of commerce. One
of the functions of a shop in People's Poland was to provide improvement: a well-designed shop 'represented the high culture of service
and aesthetics of socialist trade'.[19] Shopping was to be an elevating
and cultured experience. Inside, established forms of advertising
such as the trade-card disappeared. In its place, state offices
reminded customers of the 'correct' attitudes to consumption.
Articles appeared in the popular press criticizing 'amateur' shop
window displays, arguing that the high visibility of these 'public
galleries' made them key tools in the promotion of good taste and the
demonstration of achievement in the People's Republic.[20] 'Excess',
manifest in the pyramids of bottles and elaborate styles of display
and which had been characteristic before the war, was under prohibition. The purpose of the window was not, it was claimed, to generate
sales but to grace, like a charming still life, the monumental architecture of the new order. The aesthetics of the socialist shop window
were based on the vein of asceticism that put production first.

The political transformation from private ownership to public control was also evident in the packaging of common products. Ordinary products were branded with names and images that carried strong associations with the new regime. The popular confectioner, Wedel, which had been in business in Warsaw since 1851, was renamed Zakłady Przemysłu Cukierniczego im. '22 Lipca' (The '22 July' Confectionery Manufacturer), the date of the announcement of the People's Republic in 1944. Polish smokers could also buy 'MDM' cigarettes bearing the widely reproduced image of the monumental Socialist Realist lamps illuminating Plac Konstytucji (Constitution Square) in the capital. In such mundane ways, ideology was domesticated, and ordinary things linked to the grand cause of building socialism. MDM (Marszałkowska Dzielnica Mieszkaniowa / Marszałkowska Residential District) warrants special attention because it was presented as the paradigm for the modern, socialist townscape.

SHOPPING IN THE SQUARE

Following the announcement of a Six-Year Plan for the reconstruction of Warsaw and the introduction of an official architectural style, Socialist Realism, at a meeting of the Krajowej Partyjnej Naradzie Architektów (National Party Meeting of Architects) in Warsaw in June 1949,[21] the principal building schemes in the capital had an unmistakably political character. MDM, a scheme that combined residential buildings, an impressive square, and social agencies and services as well as shops, was particularly significant (although the full extent of the 1950–51 plan for this part of the city was never realized).[22] As an integrated district in the heart of the city, it was presented as a model – both in terms of architectural language as well as the 'socialist' distribution of space – for other urban schemes in the country. Its location, just south of the historical core of the city, and its provision of high-density accommodation as well as shops and offices had a symbolic and practical purpose: in contrast to the suburbanization of cities in Western Europe after 1945, the working classes were returned to the heart of the city – not to live in slums but in a planned and purpose-built district. MDM was planned to house 42,000 inhabitants and to operate as Poland's first 'city centre of socialist business', providing 'shops and facilities necessary for

114

the collective life of the masses'. It was to be the image of a fully integrated city, without the functional divisions between work and leisure, or culture and politics, characteristic of the West. In realizing the new socialist city, the planners intended to realize the whole socialist citizen.

Plac Konstytucji is a large square flanked by monumental buildings at the core of MDM. The ground floor of each building was occupied by shops and cafes, with apartments on the floors above. In the handsome books published to chronicle the city's apotheosis, photographic comparisons between private shops found in the city immediately before the war and those located around Plac Konstytucji became a standard feature.[23] The single-storey shacks extended by stalls that spilled out onto the streets in the 1930s were contrasted with views of the elegant, deep arcade that left the shop fascia in deep shadow, obscuring the window displays. Readers, just like the passers-by, were encouraged to admire the overall and harmonious effect of monumental classical forms rather than the goods for sale. In marked contrast to the view of street as marketplace with the disorder and hubbub that this experience entailed, Warsaw's new architecture vigilantly framed and contained the activities that it housed.

Far from being a site of consumer spectacle, MDM maintained the Stalinist fetish for production. The buildings flanking the north side of the square were given sculptural reliefs above tall ground-floor windows. In a narrative sequence, they told a story of the origins and construction of the MDM scheme itself, like Stations of the Cross. And massive figures representing generic 'positive types' associated with a productive economy, such as the miner (sculpted by Józef Gazy) and the mother (by Karol Tchorek), were set into niches along a section of the main thoroughfare running through MDM. One of the primary functions of the square as a site of consumption was subordinated to the communist mania for production.

Inside MDM's shops, the quality of design and, in particular, the fittings was patently higher than that which had been available to most private retailers in the immediate post-war period. Expensive materials such as marble, used to clad walls, as well as such opulent fittings as hand-woven carpets and candelabra lent an air of gentle luxury to the shops selling jewellery and domestic furnishings. As a mode of shopping, these retailers drew heavily upon the model of

Chimney-sweeps working on the roofs above Constitution Square, mid-1950s.

the department store: the customer, so it appeared from press reports, would be brought goods for inspection by one of the many shop assistants while waiting comfortably on one of the numerous elegant chairs. The shop's stock was not accessible: a small range of examples was placed in cabinets like museum cases for leisurely and disinterested inspection. If the department store had been a 'palace' for the middle classes in the nineteenth century affecting an image of 'opulent leisure',[24] MDM 's pretentious shops gave the impression of democratizing consumption even further across the

Sculptural relief depicting a steelworker, MDM, mid-1950s.

social scale. Even in shops selling more commonplace commodities such as food an emphatically 'kulturalny' approach to layout and retailing was envisaged. The interior of a branch of Delikatesy, frequently reproduced in propaganda in the early 1950s, was furnished with lofty classical figures flourishing symbols of bounty. At the same time, its restrained and tasteful displays of bottles of wine and other products corresponded with the vein of controlled asceticism that the state encouraged as part of its strategy of containing consumption.

Interior of a branch
of Delikatesy,
Warsaw, mid-1950s.

The democratization of luxury was rather more rhetorical than actual. Warsaw was at the heart of what a leading reform economist of the period described as a 'war economy' based on the depression of consumption. The economy during the Bierut period was based on massive investment into heavy industry; full nationalization entailing the closure of many small enterprises so that resources could be channelled into larger, 'more efficient' industrial concerns; the imposition of a new financial system controlled by a central bank, thereby keeping all investment in state hands; and, most importantly, the establishment of central-planning mechanisms, which would manage demand according to a Soviet-style 'Five-Year Plan'.[25] Like the Soviet Union in the 1930s, great emphasis was placed on rapid industrial growth in the iron and steel industries as well as in engineering. Leopold Tyrmand summed up the state of affairs in a dry observation: 'In 1950 Communism was already consuming Poland.'[26] The layout and

118

ritualized sales service of these new prestigious shops at MDM might be interpreted as not only an attempt to civilize shopping but also to control consumption. The bureaucratic process of selecting and paying for goods implied suspicion of the shopper who was unable to handle the goods without the permission of the sales assistant, as well as distrust of the staff who had to exchange receipts at each stage of the transaction: selection, payment and packaging. The transparent vitrines and elegant displays may have suggested luxury but they also masked the uneven and often insufficient supply of goods.

SHOPPING AT THE MARKET

> This buying and selling is a positive passion here – everyone
> seems obsessed by it, and the mere act of selling thrills them more
> than what they actually buy, or even what profit they make.
> Leopold Tyrmand on Warsaw's street markets in the 1950s.[27]

The state, despite its policies of nationalization, did not have a monopoly over the exchange of commodities in Warsaw. The wartime black market continued to thrive in the 1950s. Despite the uplifting rhetoric attached to Plac Konstytucji, the shadowy arcades that had been designed to contain desire provided a natural habitat for illicit trade. When vodka was in short supply in the shops or when a party ran dry at midnight, a *pół basa* (half-bottle) could always be bought at inflated prices (often in the shadowy recesses of MDM. The black market for clothes and linen was fuelled by the goods sent to Poland by relief schemes organized by Polonia (émigré Poles and their families abroad) and the United Nations Relief and Rehabilitation Administration, as well as by smuggling conducted by those fortunate to have opportunities to travel abroad. Major conduits for this illicit trade were Warsaw's street markets, particularly the Różycki Bazaar and 'Ciuchy' (slang for clothes) on Plac Szembeka at the periphery of the city. While the former included some fixed stalls, 'Ciuchy' was a more informal system with sellers staking a claim on a patch of ground on which to spread their wares. Tyrmand, the diarist, was a habitué of Warsaw's markets. After visiting the Różycki Bazaar in March 1954, he described it as 'the last true, red-blooded reserve of commercial life in Warsaw, a reserve of Warsaw humour

Cartoon by Jerzy Zaruba alluding to the black market operating in MDM in the late 1950s.

and petty villainy.'[28] Although selling and buying on the black market were prohibited, such street markets were tolerated because, like a safety valve, they satisfied demands that Polish industry could not. (And, in fact, a network of shops known as 'Komisy' was established later to combat black-market trade. Poles could legitimately sell clothes and other valuable goods, usually received from relatives abroad, through these state shops.)

Before 1956 Warsaw's street markets were usually the subject of negative comment in the press: one typical report mocked 'the offal of a transatlantic culture' on sale.[29] The failure of the state to meet the needs of consumers became a legitimate subject of public debate – a discussion licensed by destalinization – and a spate of articles appeared reporting the popularity of the 'department store under open skies' in the spirit of social investigation.[30] In December 1956 a particularly uninhibited article on 'Ciuchy' appeared in *Przekrój* (Profile), an illustrated weekly reporting culture and fashion.[31] Its author, after acknowledging the twin embarrassments that not only were the goods on sale originally sent as aid, but that Polish manufacturers could not produce such things, offered a thoughtful analysis of the motivations of shoppers. Shopping was a qualitatively different experience at 'Ciuchy' compared to that promoted by

NR 609 • CENA 1.10 ZŁ • 9 GRUDNIA 1956 ROKU

Korespondencje: Olgierda Budrewicza z Belgii, Zygmunta Broniarka z Indii i Andrzeja Klominka z Włoch ● *Monte Cassino* Melchiora Wańkowicza ● Z uczuciem i na wesoło o *Gałczyńskim* pisze S. Czejka-Stachowicz ● Krótkie opowiadanie Françoise Sagan ● *W „Modzie"* sekret spódnicy podkowy ● *Rozmaitości*

NA ZDJĘCIU: damskie i męskie, stare i nowe, modne i niemodne buty na jednym ze stoisk warszawskiej tandety. Fotoreportaż z placu Szembeka i felieton B-ci ROJEK o ciuchach znajdziecie na str. 8—9. — Fot. R. BURZYŃSKI

Cover of *Przekrój*, December 1956. The caption to the cover shot reads 'Men and women's, old and new, fashionable and unfashionable shoes on a shoddy Warsaw stall'.

the state-shop because it was based on different values. Not only did the street market offer the opportunity to engage the senses in direct and prohibited ways – fingers to touch, eyes to range over and compare all the goods on display – but it was also an 'adventure' made up of chance encounters with things. Chance, it seemed, had been extinguished by the meticulous, if flawed, scope of the Plan. The fact that many of these things came from 'beyond the iron curtain' added to their appeal as 'forbidden fruit': 'Obviously, a Czechoslovak or Bulgarian thing cannot be "ciuchy". They may be good products but they are bought with reason and not from love.' The archetypal example of 'ciuchy', for this author, involved military fatigues on which American soldiers had painted cryptic military letters and numbers. Such commodities carried a mysterious and illicit charge. For these reasons, he claimed that the official network of 'Komisy' 'could never replace the street-market even if they were improved by people attentive to the "kulturalny" . . . appearance of the city and if leading heroes of the class war replaced the grannies selling nylon knickers . . .'.

For Tyrmand, writing in 1954 before critical social comment could be freely vented, the goods available at 'Ciuchy' were a distinct and unmistakable feature of Warsaw life:

> It is paradoxical that Prague and Budapest, two intact cities with an excellent supply of clothing factories, appear less elegant than Warsaw. Of course, it is clear that the general state of dress of the crowds on the streets is incomparably higher but in Warsaw you can see a few people, chiefly young university students, dressed in a specific 'ciuchy' style thereby giving Warsaw's streets the colour of European chic. The young, without regard for 'the march of society', are the most fervent carriers of 'ciuchy' elegance. Amongst the young, socks with coloured stripes are a uniform and, at the same time, a manifesto. With these socks the young engage in a heroic battle with communist schools, with communist youth organisations, with the whole communist system. These socks stand in recent years as the sign of a holy war over the right to have your own taste . . .[32]

Striped socks had a synechdochical relationship to an entire taste culture that Tyrmand later described as 'applied fantastic'.[33] This strange compound inferred both commitment, in the effort required to produce the intended effect, and escape, in the pursuit of exotic style. Fantasy was measured by the cultural and material austerity of post-war life, as well as the political charge attached to consumption. The diverse range of clothes and other goods at 'Ciuchy' constituted, for Tyrmand, a *style*, not in terms of design or manufacture but in the manner of their consumption. Moreover, consumption was interpreted as resistance. In Bierut's Poland 'ciuchy' was not only condemned but, as we have seen, consumption itself was critically circumscribed by what Tyrmand called a 'spartan ideology'. The example of 'Ciuchy' would seem to illustrate Katherine Verdery's observation that:

> The arousal and frustration of consumer desire and East Europeans' consequent resistance to their regimes led them to build their social identities specifically *through consuming*. Acquiring consumer goods and objects conferred an identity that set one off from socialism. To acquire objects became a way of constituting your selfhood against a regime you despised.[34]

When Poland was cast in opposition to the consumer society, 'Ciuchy' provided the means for this kind of resistance. However, during the Thaw official attitudes to consumption became both more encouraging and more ambiguous at the same time.

LIFE AFTER DARK

Warsaw in the socialist future, as embodied in the form of Constitution Square, was to be *without* what the American urban historian Lewis Mumford calls 'the deepened collective anxieties', that is, the apprehension, hostility and struggle that characterize urban life.[35] Mumford's estimation of the modern metropolis as a kind of fraught and at the same time dynamic, exciting and even erotically charged space has been shared by many others. Czesław Miłosz, in his explosive demolition of the dissimulations of intellectual life in Bierut's Poland, described the urban environment as an adventure and an assault on all the senses. Describing Paris, the city where he wrote *The Captive Mind*, he found that:

> The majority find pleasure . . . in the mere fact of their existence within the stream of life. In the cities, the eye meets the colourful

store displays, the diversity of human types. Looking at the passers-by, one can guess from their faces the story of their lives. This movement of the imagination when a man is walking through a crowd has an erotic tinge; his emotions are very close to psychological sensations. He rejoices in dresses, in the flash of lights; while for instance, Parisian markets with their heaps of vegetables and flowers, fish of every shape and hue, sides of meat dripping with every shade of red offer delights, he need not go seeking them in Dutch or Impressionist painting. He hears snatches of arias, the throbbing of motors mixed with the warble of birds, called greetings, laughter. His nose is assailed by changing odours: coffee, gasoline, oranges, ozone, roasting nuts, perfumes.[36]

Warsaw by contrast seemed oppressively predictable. It lacked the excitement and sensual range that other cities in Western Europe offered their visitors. Miłosz did not feel alone in his opinion, describing a widespread 'hunger for strangeness'. Leopold Tyrmand used his diary as an outlet for those views that did not meet the censor's approval. His opinion of MDM in 1954, originally penned for *Tygodnik Powszechny*, appeared in his private journal. Like Miłosz he was repelled by the dreary vision of the city projected in what he called the garb of 'emdeemizm' (MDM-ism):

> Monotonous, identical, gigantic, flat boxes with columns, turrets and allegorical figures will extend greatest Warsaw's streets for kilometres. No one who has seen these designs, will be able to imagine himself in this monotonous and appallingly boring place . . . These buildings will provide apartments, offices and hotels. Yet it is impossible to imagine them bearing neon signs, advertisements or any individual accent . . . Desperate post-war antagonisms have produced this ridiculous and ugly place. When every chemists, boutique and confectioners shares the same, uniform appearance, we will have fallen into chaos and nonsense.[37]

Tyrmand did not have to wait long for the change in political climate that allowed similar views of MDM to be expressed in public. The Thaw gave licence to criticize the flaws of Socialist Realist architecture and to begin exploring the expressive and technical potential of modern architecture. MDM was singled out for its lifelessness. If Warsaw lacked the stimulating vibrancy of the modern capitalist city, then the solution seemed clear: Warsaw should adopt some of its defining features. Jerzy Wierzbicki wrote: 'Note the absence of advertising, lighting and neon: the elements which in the evening hours lend great liveliness and diversity to a city. The city centre must be a concentration of hotels, restaurants, cafés, travel offices, attractive shop premises. The life of a great city presses for them . . .'.[38]

One of the first signs of a shift in urban aesthetics was the wave of neon signs that were fixed to the city's buildings in the late 1950s. For some commentators, neon was a quick remedy for the dead spaces of MDM and, with this in mind, a 'campaign' to 'neonize' the city was inaugurated by *Stolica*, a popular magazine. The illuminated lettering and dancing symbols announcing the appearance of Cocktail, a new café, or Szanghaj, a Chinese restaurant, introduced a new cosmopolitan vocabulary. This was, of course, a form of advertising, a phenomenon which had been under prohibition only a few years earlier (and never really shook off the odour of exploitation in the People's Republic). The neon signs, however, demonstrated sufficient restraint to be accommodated. Like signposts, these new brilliant torches in the cityscape were useful landmarks with which to navigate an expanding city. Fixed and unchanging, they did not encourage the voracious cycle of fashion on which capitalism thrived. The illuminated images and words that appeared above the streets were matter-of-fact, denoting a commodity or service ('Save with PKO for your apartment') rather than the seductions of what one Polish commentator later called the 'Alice in Wonderland' world of advertising in the West.[39]

The practical value of neon was rather over-stressed by its advocates in the press, keen not to be seen as closet-capitalists. But it has to be said that the neon lightscape – a nocturnal spectacle drawing the citizenry back into the city after their daily toils – suggested life after dark. Unlike the propaganda campaign that promised the return of the working class back to the city centre during the Bierut era, neon was not an invitation to an ordered city. Light and dark were lent unambiguous, somewhat banal, values during the Stalin period. The city at night was typically represented as a threatening place, stirring fears of criminality and anti-social behaviour. In Aleksander Ford's 1954 film *Five from Barska Street*, a powerful and

Neon on Warsaw's streets, 1958.

moving account of Warsaw in the late 1940s, a gang of young men, psychologically and physically damaged by war and manipulated by anti-communist agitators, use the cover of night – shot in thick, oily tones – to hide their lawlessness. The agent of their deliverance is the city itself. Working as members of the building crews on one of the great new building projects, the East–West Thoroughfare under the Old Town, they come to understand their offences. A few years later, in a shift towards the greater cultural complexity that characterized the Thaw period, film-makers could find a wider range of meanings in the image of the city at night. Andrzej Wajda's neglected 1960 film *Niewinni czarodzieje* (Innocent Sorcerers) adopts Warsaw's shadowy jazz clubs and inky black streets, lit only by neon signs and the light cast from shop windows, as its *mise-en-scène*. A love story without moral censure or an overtly political message, Wajda's film represents Warsaw, recognizable by his use of actual streets and already legendary jazz clubs, as a place of adventure and pleasure.

Although displaying little ideological rectitude (unlike the political slogans strung across streets at the time of Party congresses), neon – for all its associations with pleasure – did have its political merits. In its suggestive modernity, neon symbolized new promises about the way in which life was going to be improved. A reform leadership under Gomułka introduced a partial market economy in 1957 with the intention of increasing the production of consumer goods. The strategy of introducing greater flexibility and decentralization in industrial production had the effect of encouraging Polish manufacturers to compete. Reform economists now argued for profit – only a few months earlier a wretched offence against the working class – as a measure by which productivity could be gauged. Although the state continued to subscribe to central planning as well as national ownership of the means of production, an element of pluralism entered into economic life, not least in the form of private businesses such as taxi services and restaurants. A new emphasis was put on pleasure and leisure. The 'standard of living', always an ambiguous concept, was now being defined materially rather than in terms of education, political consciousness or, as the Stalinists had viewed it, culture. The neon sign flashing the English word 'Cocktail' onto Warsaw's streets was meant to be seen as a vivid sign of the times.

A qualification needs to be made here. The material world actually changed rather slowly during the Thaw and, in any case, much slower than the iconographic one of adverts, films and magazines. Consumer goods only trickled onto the market in the late 1950s and early 1960s in a slow drip making little impact on people's lives. By contrast, *images* of consumption expanded exponentially during this time. Magazine and newspaper editors were no longer under pressure to represent the world outside exclusively in terms of Cold War polarities. Events and patterns of life, whether fashion from France or American jazz, could now be reported in the spirit of social documentary. The pre-war magazine *Dookoła świata* (Around the World) was revived by the ZMP in January 1954 with this intention: Tyrmand called it a 'concession' made by the regime (a type of commodity that the Eastern Bloc specialized in producing).[40] Until October 1959, when the Central Committee castigated such popular magazines for exhibiting uncritical enthusiasm for 'Western culture',[41] they were important channels presenting a picture of modern affluence. Similarly, from 1956 American and Western European films were

'Śródmieście', a temporary covered market designed in 1957 by Tadeusz Tomicki and Ryszard Trzaska on Marszałkowska Street, 1957.

widely distributed, attracting much higher audiences than East European imports.[42] Against a flood of images of life in the West, a number of Stalinist shibboleths were depoliticized: shopping and consumption in general were increasingly associated with pleasure and, by the same process, leisure was released from the improving sphere of 'kulturalny' activity. Articles appeared in the press on shopping as an enjoyable and leisurely occupation;[43] advertising returned to the pages of popular magazines and, of course, neon flickered into life on the streets of Warsaw. Consumption – if only in terms of images – was no longer a threat to socialist society, it was part of its promise.

NEW SHOPS

Against the background of an efflorescence of images of consumption, the shop was reassessed by architects and urban planners, particularly in Warsaw, the most prestigious site of state activity. The

128

'Supersam', Puławska Street, designed by Jerzy Hryniewiecki, Maciej Krasiński and Ewa Krasińska, 1959.

new economic model encouraged private shops and kiosks. State-owned retailers also expanded during the late 1950s to sell the new consumer goods manufactured by state enterprises as well as imports.[44] According to Hansjakob Stehle, writing in 1965, the proliferation of new retailers brought about the demise of the street market.[45] In fact, the market lived on, not least in the modes of selling adopted by Warsaw's new shops. One of the earliest examples of these new structures was the temporary building designed in 1957 by Tadeusz Tomicki and Ryszard Trzaska for the Stołeczny Zarząd Handlu on Marszałkowska Street, close to MDM. This steel-framed and glass-walled 'pavilion', called 'Śródmieście' (City centre), accommodated 42 private stalls selling clothes and household goods. A modernist box deposited on the paving stones, Śródmieście was fronted with glass, giving the impression of projecting the goods for sale into the street. At night this glass box was illuminated from within so that the skeletal structure almost disappeared and the merchandise appeared to be suspended in the light. Such shops were increasingly conceived as part of an urban spectacle offering diversity and surprise.[46] Architects and planners conceiving new schemes in Warsaw imagined lively streets filled with bright shops and flanked with billboards. The unacknowledged though obvious source for this conception of the urban environment was the capitalist city.

Another novelty on Warsaw's streets imported from the West was the supermarket, the most conspicuous example being 'Supersam' at the start of Puławska Street, designed in 1959 by Jerzy Hryniewiecki, Maciej Krasiński and Ewa Krasińska. This landmark building was a dramatic statement of faith on the part of architects and the authorities in a technologically determined conception of modernity: in the use of 'industrial' materials such as reinforced concrete; and in ostentatious structural forms, such as the cantilevered concrete canopy over the entrance and the dramatically cambered beams that spanned the brightly lit shopping hall. The shift towards self-service associated with the 'open shop' was understood as empowering consumers in that they were now able to judge goods in hitherto prohibited ways. (This idea caused some controversy: some state retailers, fearful of theft and breakage, called for programmes to educate consumers in this new 'culture' of shopping.)[47] Shelves were to be stacked high with products giving the unmistakable impression of profusion. The supermarket, as a style of retailing, was evidently not modelled on Soviet precedents but American ones. During the period of destalinization, and following Khrushchev's lead in the Soviet Union, America could be characterized in new, more moderate ways. The fact, for instance, that the ideological and economic outlook of the two countries was polarized became less important than the usefulness of the technical knowledge that the American building industry could supply. Thus, the supermarket was presented (not least by technocrats such as architects) as a quintessentially modern development and, as such, one which the communists were compelled to introduce to Poland. Warsaw, it seemed in the late 1950s, was being remade in the image of the consumer society. In this aspect of life – as others – the communists modulated their claim about the unique and superior nature of the socialist system.

130

Tadeusz Kędzielski, customer: In the window there are various cheeses on display. But in the shop there are none to be bought. For what reason has it become customary to advertise goods which are unavailable in the shop? Please answer me.

Shop-manager: The shop is taking part in a display competition ... Such goods have unfortunately not been available for sale for a long time.

Entry and response in the comments book of a Warsaw branch of Sp0łem, 1983.[48]

The 'self-image' of socialism in Poland changed dramatically during the Thaw. Despite his personal reputation for asceticism, Gomułka's regime encouraged the Poles to think of themselves as consumers. By constantly raising expectations of improved standards of living, socialism in Poland aroused desire. Moreover, as the economy failed, year in year out, to meet its promises, people grew increasingly frustrated. In Katherine Verdery's words, 'in socialism desire floated free in endless search of goods people saw as their right'.[49] Protest about supply and cost of even the most essential items became a marked feature of Polish political life from the late 1960s (as, in fact, it had been in the early 1950s). Workers' grievances about the cost of living made the communist leadership apprehensive, with good reason. When the Polish food manufacturing industry failed to meet its quotas, as regularly was the case in the 1960s and '70s, the authorities resorted to massive price rises to stem demand. In the winter of 1970/71 steep price rises triggered strikes along the Baltic coast that, after a number of workers died in clashes with the security forces, resulted in Gomułka's fall from power. By manufacturing a boom with money borrowed from the West and keeping the cost of food to Polish consumers down with subsidies, Gierek, his successor, fared a little better. For a short period it seemed that his plans for a 'great leap forward', which would turn Poland into a net exporter, was succeeding. Shops filled with new consumer goods and the standard of living rose. Many prices, particularly of symbolic goods like meat and bread, were kept artificially at 1965 levels as a sop to public opinion. But when in 1976 his administration was forced to announce dramatic price increases to cope with what was an inevitable crisis, violent demonstrations ignited around the country, most notoriously in Radom, but also at the Ursus tractor plant in Warsaw (an important symbol of modern socialist industry). The repression that followed in Radom – first meted out with clubs and then by the withdrawal of funds for social services – was the trigger for the formation of KOR (see chapter One). Fearful of further unrest, authority lost control of the economy and struggled to repay the enormous debts owed to the West. Polish manufactured goods were often shoddy and, as such, difficult to export. To raise revenue, the only choice was to sell coal and other raw materials. In the winter of 1978/9 the Poles froze in their offices and homes as power stations ran out of fuel. Unable to renew its manufacturing infrastructure, industry could not produce even basic items like matches and cigarettes. Like a motor with worn cogs, Poland seemed to be grinding to a halt.

The only thing being produced in Poland at this time, it seemed, was the queue. Queues were an inescapable feature of city life, except for the few. Those who had access to foreign currency could shop for imported goods on the well-stocked shelves of the many PEWEX shops (another Gierek innovation, these 'internal export' shops selling imported alcohol, textiles, medicine and even cars were introduced to tap reserves of hard currency under Polish mattresses). The majority joined the long snaking lines of frustrated shoppers outside shops, formed sometimes on the basis of no more than a rumour of a delivery. Despite the lame excuses claiming 'temporary difficulties' in the supply of materials (and in 1980–81, when Solidarity was at its height, the official complaint that the opposition had brought the economy to crisis), everything seemed to be in short supply, whether basic staples or luxury items. Like some kind of perverse communist utopia, money became almost worthless as barter and the reciprocation of favours (*kombinacja*) became the primary means of exchange.

The queue was the inevitable symbol of the age. Adopted as a trope by a number of writers, the image of a society lined up in immeasurable queues symbolized the absurdity of life. In Tadeusz Konwicki's novel *Kompleks Polski* (The Polish Complex, 1977) the 147 people in a queue outside a Jubiler (state-run jewellers), waiting on Christmas Eve for a delivery of gold rings from the Soviet Union, include a writer, a plainclothes policeman and a professional queuer. They are joined by a group of Soviet citizens who have come to Poland as 'suitcase traders', tourists who purchase goods abroad to sell on their return. Some of the queuers – including the author – have met before. Konwicki at the beginning of his career in the 1940s had been an enthusiastic Socialist Realist writer, lending his literary talents to the cause of building socialism. In this autobiographical fantasy, he tells the tale of an assassin once sent by the anti-communist resistance to silence him. In turn the assassin is being tailed, 'Indian file' like the queue, by a secret policeman. These three figures come, bound together again by fate, to find themselves in line waiting for Soviet gold thirty years later. Now drained of any ideological fervour, they share the same absurdly 'democratic' end; to stand in a queue waiting for something that will not arrive.[50] Konwicki's novel was banned, not least because it emphasized the gulf between rhetoric and experience. 'Temporary difficulties' of this sort had lasted for thirty years (and were to persist for another dozen or so). Publishing this novel as a samizdat book was, as Stanisław Barańczak argued, Konwicki's refusal to sink into silent acceptance of absurdity.

At about the same time Václav Havel, in his essay 'The Power of the Powerless', employed not the queue but the figure of the shop-keeper to trace the false threads that bound society to what he called post-totalitarian authority. By unthinkingly displaying banal party slogans in the window alongside his carrots and onion, the shop-keeper was not signalling his ardour for socialism:

> The real meaning of the greengrocer's slogan has nothing to do with what the text of the slogan actually says. Even so, this real meaning is quite clear and generally comprehensible because the code is so familiar: the greengrocer declares his loyalty in the only way the regime is capable of hearing; that is, by accepting the prescribed ritual, by accepting the appearances as reality, by accepting the rules of the game. In doing so, he has become a player in the game, thus making it possible for the game to go on . . .[51]

Havel articulated the central themes in many of the protests of the anti-communist intelligentsia, that of the dignity of the individual and the imperative of living in truth. Authority and ideology had been internalized so that, while 'post-totalitarian' power had recourse to force, it did not need to use it. Ordinary people in their everyday lives 'confirm the system, fulfil the system, make the system, *are* the system'.

Window of a Monopol, the state alcohol retailer, Warsaw, 1975.

During the economic collapse of the late 1970s and the 1980s, grocers' shop windows in Warsaw often had nothing more to offer than banal ideological slogans and wan paper flags. The opening phrase of the motto of the *Communist Manifesto*, 'Workers of the World Unite', may well have brought to mind the words that followed, 'You have nothing to lose . . .', when it appeared in a vacant shop window. Moreover, the practice of mounting window displays of mundane goods – piles of greasy soap and jars of thin mayonnaise – that were unavailable for purchase enraged would-be customers, whose angry complaints filled the book that each shop had to keep for this purpose.[52]

Sometimes the kind of amateurish displays suggested more than the hollow conformity described by Havel. In 1975 the window-dresser of one Warsaw Monopol (State Alcohol Retailer) lined up a dozen or more empty vodka bottles, perhaps surveying the brands that might be purchased inside. However, the poster behind, promoting a film celebrating 'Our Journey over Thirty Years' (i.e., the thirtieth anniversary of the People's Republic of Poland), hinted at another view of the Poles' feats in these decades, not least the widespread taste for the 'hydraulic breakfast' of vodka. Although the authorities regularly mounted campaigns against alcoholic excess, many Poles – including perhaps the person who dressed this window – viewed the widespread availability of vodka and 'spiritus', a mind-damaging 97 per cent proof spirit, as a sign of state duplicity. After the imposition of martial law, the Church-led opposition interpreted the availability of vodka as part of a strategy of subjugation. Kazimierz Brandys put it bluntly in 1984: 'Russia is infiltrating us in a different way than thirty-five years ago . . . via vodka, via corruption and bribery.'[53] The 'crystal spirit' symbolized not socialism so much as Poland's drift eastwards into what many Poles saw as a state of *un*civilization. In a society long versed in what has been called the 'spirit of metaphor', a shop window could be a site of social and political comment.[54]

Warsaw's shops in the 1980s, like the entire country, seemed to petrify. Few new stores were built, leaving the barren housing estates on the city's fringes poorly served. The modern stores that had once seemed so striking when they opened their doors in the 1960s were decaying. Rusting and moulding, their open structures and abstract mosaics revealed the system's inability to rejuvenate itself. If the neon signs, escalators and refrigerators worked, they emitted a fatal buzzing like a Geiger counter. Shop windows were left unchanged for months, the dusty displays slowly bleaching and curling in the sunlight. Outside, the advertisements that had been painted in the 1960s on the ends of Warsaw's tenements took on the quaint appearance of relics from more optimistic times. Ad hoc rearrangement of the retail space, often in ways that perverted the original architectural concept, seemed to obstruct shoppers. A number of the large department stores in the centre of the city, including the strikingly modernist CDT on Aleje Jerozolimskie (today Smyk, a children's clothing and toy store), constructed along Corbusian lines in the late 1940s, took openness as its design principle. In the 1980s all bar one of the bank of glass doors designed to invite the shopper inside were invariably locked. In winter this sole opening was shrouded with a thick, damp worsted veil to keep the cold out. Inside, the open floors, which had been designed to allow shoppers to inspect the stock, were partitioned and closed off with rudimentary barriers. Often a large crowd pressed into makeshift

Advertising for Orbis, the state travel agency, Warsaw, photographed in the mid-1980s.

corridors straining to see what could be purchased, while the shop assistant floated in an open and often empty space. The control over the movement of customers as well as the indifference to matters of display and service marked an absolute low. Making no pretence to the luxury of the department store or to the suggestion of choice associated with the supermarket, these shops offered no dissimulation. They were the gaunt face of an economy too long on the verge of breakdown.

STREETS AND MARKETS

If what and where to buy had been the pressing questions of the 1980s, the issue of what and where to sell seemed to occupy many Varsovians in the 1990s. Even before the dissolution of the Soviet Bloc, the Poles had acquired a reputation as budding entrepreneurs who used tourist visas to engage in 'suitcase trading'. When visa-free travel to Germany became possible after the fall of the Wall, thousands of would-be entrepreneurs established what were often rather grandiosely known as 'Import-Export' businesses. Warsaw's new merchants would fill their small Fiats with videos, cooking oil or other consumer goods in Berlin and return to Poland to sell these 'imports' on the streets. Polish-made goods, which generally had low reputations, were passed over by knowing consumers in favour of a vast wave of imported products, available in increasing numbers.

Furthermore, this situation in the capital was exacerbated when, in 1990, it became a huge, sprawling street-market of Polish and Soviet traders. The parks at the foot of the Palace of Culture and Science became an enormous and chaotic bazaar with people selling from the back of trucks and from plastic sheets spread on the ground. Goods seemed to have been spilled onto its wide and ordered streets as if tipped from the air. As the Soviet Union crumbled, its impoverished citizens would travel from as far as Baku and Tashkent to sell anything that might have a market value. The plastic toys, nylon-rich clothes and packets of crumbling cigarettes on these stalls represented the pathetic material failure of Soviet industry. The zloties for which these things were sold could then be converted into precious hard currency. Their coach journey could take up to two weeks across the Soviet Union and days on the border. Nevertheless, it was clearly worthwhile: thirty dollars profit was then the equivalent of more than six months' average wages. Warsaw became in the course of just a few months a 'trade centre' in ways hardly envisaged by the monetarists newly taking their seats in the Polish parliament. Evidently, when the Poles voted for the politics of the market in the momentous elections of June 1989, they quite literally got markets.

In autumn 1991 the Mayor of Warsaw, under pressure from President Wałęsa, sent the police with water-cannons to wash the vendors from the city streets. The sellers may have been regarded as unsightly and suspicious by the new political class, particularly those who had viewed the overthrow of communist authority in idealistic terms, but they serviced real needs. Their appeal was not simply a matter of cost. Grey streets seemed to acquire new colour by their presence. In a city, for instance, which had no more than a handful of expensive Chinese restaurants beyond the price range of most legally earned wages, the arrival of dozens of Vietnamese stalls selling cheap food offered exciting, new sensations. There was

Kiosks erected in Constitution Square in the early 1990s.

ideological symbolism in the street market too. The course of 'shock treatment' recommended by World Bank monetarists in the early 1990s promised reward after pain. The mythical appeal of capitalism lay in its transformatory effects: unfettered business could make millionaires. To curb street trading was to snuff out this dream. As a conciliatory gesture to this growing merchant class and the market they served, the city erected massive, tent-like markets in the grounds of the Palace of Culture to house small stalls – an echo of 'Śródmieście', the 1960 pavilion, which had been sited only a few hundred metres away. The demand for new shop premises also encouraged the city authorities to tender for offers to manage street markets at focal points in the city. This was an attempt to control the business culture of the city, which, at that time, was an unregulated, raw form of capitalism. The city stipulated that these schemes utilize temporary structures (i.e. kiosks), which could be rented by small businesses. Administered and regulated, traders would be responsible for the goods that they sold.

Elsewhere in the city street vending was corralled rather than 'improved' by the spaces it occupied. Stadion Dziesięciolecia, the sports stadium on the right bank of the Vistula, fell into disrepair in the 1970s as the Polish economy slid into decline. In 1989 it became the site of an enormous sprawling market, which adopted the name Jarmark Europa (Europe's Fair). While the centre of the amphi-

138

theatre was abandoned, like a classical ruin, the brim of the bowl and the paths that lead up to it were packed with up to 4,000 traders, large numbers coming from Vietnam, Africa, Russia and the Middle East. The goods on sale often had dubious pedigrees, many being pirate copies of branded goods or adulterated products like whisky and vodka 'thinned' with uncertain liquids. Like a perverse coincidence of history, this was the second time that the 'global village' has come to this particular site. In 1955 the newly opened stadium had been the host venue of the International Festival of Youth. For a few days it became a vividly multicultural city welcoming 30,000 guests from 114 countries to march for peace and sing folk-songs. Today, the stadium has become the most multicultural space in the city again. It represents a form of globalization 'from below' that is slowly changing the city's make-up.[55] The Poles' relations with these new arrivals in the city are ambiguous. The large Vietnamese community, estimated at 30,000, complain that they suffer harassment from officials and neighbours while stalls run by Poles nearby are unmolested.[56] At the same time, their presence reminds the Poles of their own recent past as 'suitcase traders' in Western Europe.

Relatively unregulated, the stadium and other informal stalls clustered around the bus stops and suburban railway stations have been far more popular with the population than the city authorities. When in 2001 a market research company researched opinion of different retail spaces in Poland, the greatest enthusiasts for markets were to be found in Warsaw: 70 per cent of the city's population shopped in these places. Nevertheless, Mayor Paweł Piskorski promised to 'liquidate' the stadium and build a new market hall with private finance for 600 stalls.[57] While this hostility is in part to do with regulating the circulation of sometimes dangerous goods that pay no regard to patents and copyright, and the pressure exerted by investors building new shopping centres, it also reflects a desire to sharpen the identity of the city. For some commentators, even those who have much to gain from the expansion of the city, such as architects, Warsaw has been blurred by the sprawl and noise of the market. Others, making veiled reference to a kind of ethnic discourse, talk about the need to restore the city's European face. Playing upon a deeply entrenched view of the backwardness of the East (whether a Soviet occident or a more loosely Asian one), the market appears to threaten the long promised aim of 'rejoining Europe', whether in some general sense of way of living or more particularly as a member of the EU. Commentators in the press ask whether the stadium and other market halls could be 'civilized', a word with more associations with the church and museum than the street. Similarly, legislation was passed in 2002 that prohibited the import of second-hand clothing from abroad, much of it sold on Warsaw's stalls. The authors of this law, designed in the first instance to protect the country's struggling clothing producers, described it as an attempt to 'civilize the clothing market'.[58] 'Civilized' consumption is, in fact, a new rendition of an old tune, that of 'kulturalny' consumption. To those who use the term, it suggests a world where the market is contained by civic values. Just as the buildings around Constitution Square in the mid-1950s were designed to moderate the commercial spectacle, architecture is being invoked again as a means of regulation, containing the viral spread and visual pollution of the market.

In post-communist discourse, street markets are not by definition uncivilized places. Claimed to be a characteristic feature of 'authentic' Warsaw life before and during socialism, their supporters suggest that the longest established spaces have a 'heritage' value. Of 'Koszyki', a steel-framed and glass-roofed market hall of 1906–9, one writer recently stressed that:

> Koszykowa Hall is a part of Old Warsaw which today finds itself in a catastrophic state. Its significance comes not just from the fact that it survived the bombardment but that it manifests old splendour (świetność). It should connect the old with the new, and good traditions of trade with modern life.[59]

With similar intent, the Różycki Bazaar in the Praga district celebrated its one hundred and first anniversary in 2002 with a carousel, *flaki* (tripe) and beer. As shoppers tested their strength on a vintage 'bomba', a street band with accordion, violin and guitar played the street songs of the local Praga district, a much mythologized and popular musical genre. Warsaw was nostalgically transported back to an idealized past, where the black market was a kind of lifeline to colour and criminality was mere 'roguishness'. In organizing this event, members of the Różycki Bazaar Traders' Association sought to lend their businesses incontrovertible historical value (as well as draw custom away from the shopping

140

malls). While the communists found it difficult to absorb 'authentic' working-class patterns of life into the cultural forms it sanctioned, capitalism seems to have little problem doing so.

To conclude this tour of shops and markets over the last fifty years, let's return to Constitution Square. Designed as a kind of urban prototype for the great social revolution, it has been the testing ground for many of the new businesses that have been formed since 1989. In fact, the changes in its appearance over the last fifteen years are like a condensed version of the themes of this chapter. In the early 1990s its great expanse was filled with a sprawling shanty town of traders. To contain this unregulated market, small red and white kiosks – sometimes housing fast food restaurants skirted with white fences and plastic garden furniture for al fresco meals – were installed by the city authorities. The grand shops behind changed profile as the state-owned retailers scaled down their operations and smart car showrooms and up-market electrical retailers moved in. A long empty island at the centre of the square, formed by the flow of traffic, was adopted as a car park. By the end of the decade attempts to install three-storey video screens to broadcast adverts into this busy and disordered space prompted the city authorities to act, encouraged by critics who saw street trading as a form of urban blight. Some spoke up for a stronger role for authority, arguing that the market needs regulation, whereas others were motivated by urban aesthetics, finding Warsaw's new capitalist guise ugly and chaotic. (Fast food chains and supermarkets have largely escaped critical comment precisely because they offer the kind of order and control that both desire, even if urban aesthetes take little pleasure in their design.) As the 1990s drew to a close, plans were announced for the improvement of the square. As a result, Constitution Square has, it seems, been slowly returned to its original form. Care has been taken to keep the original decorative scheme with its Stalinist imagery, while the commercial ornaments have been pruned. Improvements include changes to the flow of traffic through what remains a busy square and resurfacing extended pedestrian areas with pretty block-work. Above all, the site has been cleared of traces of 'undignified' street trading, described as 'straganiarstwo' (huck-sterism) in the press. One form of street selling has been replaced with another, apparently more cultured. In the summer the broad paving flanking the square is occupied with outdoor cafés selling cappuccinos and bottled beer. As one report in the Warsaw press makes clear in its title, 'Over Tankards on Constitution Square', the appearance of beer in the symbolic home of Polish socialism signals more than just the pleasures of a drink: it is a victory in the campaign (waged by the breweries, among others) to persuade the Poles to abandon their attachment to vodka.[60] Beer is made to symbolize Poland's return to Western 'civilization', whereas 'Eastern' vodka suggests Poland's long captivity by Imperial Russia and the Soviet Union. It seems that the Square's original function, as a site of improvement, has been revived, albeit in a post-communist mode. To drink a bottled beer served by a waiter in a white apron in a new café in a restored Constitution Square, overlooked by the heroes of labour and Stakhanovite workers, is to toast the defeat of the brand of socialism that once ruled Warsaw *and* the containment of the market.

III At Home in the City

In the period of 'normalization' following the repeal of martial law in the mid-1980s, Jerzy Urban was probably the most hated man in Poland. The government spokesman appeared on television almost every day to berate his viewers for 'blindly' following the 'foolhardy' lead of the Solidarity opposition. Urban, today a publisher who regularly features in lists of 'Poland's Richest Men', had then, as now, a special talent for derision. In the mid-1980s he started a campaign to collect blankets for the homeless living on the streets in New York. Pity the poor of the capitalist system, he argued, for they do not enjoy the protection available to the citizen of socialist Poland. To most of his compatriots Urban's appeal seemed pure malice. One only had to walk through Warsaw's main streets to see the ashen effects of poverty. The underground newspaper *Samorządna Rzeczpospolita* in January 1988 took homelessness as a sign of the system's impending breakdown:

> Several decades ago they were one of those rarely encountered elements of city folklore. They were usually from the margins of society: alcoholics, aged prostitutes, the mentally subnormal, or people without families. Today, there are many of them, more and more each month. They are 'divers', people who search in city garbage cans for things to eat, wear or sell. 'Divers' of the old category are hardly ever seen today. The garbage cans today are frequented by people who look as though they could be members of the intelligentsia . . . When their coat and their last pair of shoes are finally worn out and they do not have enough money to replace them, people who until recently would never have dreamt of it, overcome their feelings of disgust and shame and will set off for the garbage cans.[1]

In the image-world of state socialism, homelessness only existed in the callous West, yet it was a familiar and persistent feature of life.

Warsaw has faced a perpetual shortage of living space. Even before the Second World War the city's housing stock was never adequate. Today, despite the fact that the population is shrinking (it reached its peak in 1987 at almost 1.7 million people) and thousands of new apartments have been built, it remains one of the most poorly housed capital cities in Europe.[2] It is estimated that there is a housing shortage of 40,000 flats in the city, inhibiting diversity in household structures and limiting the mobility of the workforce.[3] High rents and low wages – as well as broad-shouldered security guards – keep these new apartment buildings 'exclusive', while the high-rise city that houses the majority decays and cracks. With the disappearance of the social system that built these tower block homes, the pull of gravity and the forces of time have taken command. The future of these buildings – worryingly augured by the fissures that have opened between the concrete panels from which they were constructed – is an issue that has yet to be addressed.

The housing problem was most acute during the 1940s and '50s when many of the people rebuilding the city and their lives were crammed, head-to-toe, into workers' hostels and communal apartments. In a poignant and funny sequence in *Skarb*, a 1949 film directed by Leonard Buczkowski, the square-jawed hero, a bus driver, makes his way from the front door in a communal apartment to his quarters. Passing through a seemingly endless enfilade of rooms formed by partitions in a once-grand flat, he encounters Polish society in the round: slumbering pensioners; a mother nursing a baby and soothing her husband's aching tooth; students reading their books; and a party celebrating a wedding, dancing a mazurka. At last he enters his own room. Yet he is still not alone, for it too is shared with another irritable bachelor. The rest of the film describes his search for a home for his new bride, the clippie on his trolleybus route. Somewhat predictably, it ends like a socialist fairy tale with the couple passing over the threshold of a new flat. Homelessness – like the ruin – could only be represented as a tragedy from which a new world was being built.

The communists put housing at the heart of their programme. It was in this field, perhaps more than in any other, that their achievements would be measured by the people they claimed to embrace. As the baton of leadership was passed within the Party, each new administration damned the failures of its predecessors and proclaimed new cause for renewed optimism. 'We will live better'

144

was a refrain crooned at every Party congress and in each five-year plan.[4] But housing demand constantly outstripped supply. While the situation was critical throughout the country, Warsaw – ravaged by war – was always recognized as rather a special case. Uniquely in Poland, for instance, the ownership of all land within the city boundaries passed to the control of the municipal authorities in 1945, and in 1949 all existing housing was taken under state control or 'communalized' (bar small, single-family homes). Five years later, controls, akin to the 'internal passport' system that operated in the Soviet Union, were introduced to stem the tide of people moving to the capital.

In the late 1950s, with a new regime at the helm, housing policy was subject to a degree of liberalization to take pressure off the city's scant resources. New co-operatives – responsible for managing and building housing estates – claimed people's savings in return for a reduced wait on the housing list. Nevertheless, it was common for newly-weds to live with their in-laws hoping that they would be able to bear the strain of waiting ten years or more for an apartment to be built. Demand was so acute that it exhausted the resources and the imagination of each successive leadership. Like tinned sardines, families were raised in small, one- or two-room apartments in which the living room doubled up as a bedroom, often for more than one generation, and the 'blind' kitchen was a windowless galley. Once secured, a home was too precious to be given up and, as a result, people rarely moved. In this context of shortage, it comes then as no surprise that Warsaw citizens watched their city rise from the ruins with more than just polite interest or civic pride. As Leopold Tyrmand remarked sardonically in his novel Zły, 'In the 'fifties everyone in Warsaw knew a little about architecture, just as everyone in the Yukon knew something about gold.'

Social housing was both instrument and emblem of the New Order. Built to standard designs with shared facilities on common land, apartment buildings were architectural declarations of social justice. Employing modern building technology (in the form of steel frames and pre-cast concrete panels) and the latest 'science' of the ergonomic kitchen or waste removal, the tall tower blocks set down in the cityscape from the early 1960s were, like the supermarkets and sports stadia at the centre, indisputable demonstrations of socialist modernity. While the architectural form of these buildings – collective and massive, like the society that they were to represent – was easily assimilated into Party discourse, the interiors that they accommodated were rather more ambiguous. Housing, after all, is not the same as homes. What interest did authority take in the interiors of these housing blocks? What constituted the right kind of interior and, by extension, the right way of living?

For much of the Cold War, the assault on privacy was a key theme in reports on life in Eastern Europe. Paranoid states that relied on surveillance and coercion, it was argued, abused 'natural' rights to privacy.[5] This was perhaps most evident during the drama of martial law in the early 1980s, when the authorities made it clear that 'private' telephone calls were being monitored and letters were stamped to show who had opened them. Privacy should, however, not just be thought about in terms of high political tension. It is as much to do with the ordinary ways in which spaces and things are appropriated, shared and individualized. The arrangement of books on a shelf or the way in which a door is pulled to can be articulations of privacy too. It is made and remade everyday in countless small acts. In this chapter, I'll explore not only the attempts to contain domestic privacy by the emaciated forms of collectivism that the communists introduced to Polish society, but also the ways after the 1950s in which privacy was increasingly encouraged in Warsaw.

Class has been both an exaggerated and at the same time an elusive aspect of Warsaw life. Although communist rhetoric turned on a stock of social caricatures, particularly during the 1950s when the steel-jawed proletarian worker and the hunched kulak were ranked to fight a 'class war', Polish society continued to attach significance to other, older patterns of distinction. Circumstances in the Polish capital lent weight to the matter of social background. Not only was the city rebuilt after the devastation of war, society had to be remade too. Few districts – largely those on the right bank of the Vistula that escaped total destruction[6] – had well-established communities attached to the districts in which they lived. Much of the population after 1944 was made up of new arrivals, coming either from the dreary Mazowsze countryside around the city, drawn by opportunity, or from other towns and cities that had been incorporated into the Soviet Union. While these new arrivals made good use of social networks that a village background offered (not least access to supplies of food when the shops ran short), they also felt the occasional glance of disdain from 'old' Warsaw. This was particularly true of some members of the intelligentsia, who, keen to demonstrate their anti-communism, would claim to detect a whiff of the farm in the new Party elite. The wife of Party leader Gierek (himself a former miner with a certain gloss lent by his fluent French and polished manners) was the butt of jokes ridiculing her airs and graces.

Housing had a key role to play in the assertion of both social and socialist identities. Districts were given over to favoured professions. Surviving 1930s apartment blocks in the streets around Jaworzyńska Street near the Zbawiciela church were, for instance, well known as police housing and, therefore, a place for *sotto voce* conversations. The prestigious apartments on the royal route along Krakowskie Przedmieście and Nowy Świat were given as grace-and-favour housing to artists, writers, actors and film and theatre directors in the 1950s. As I'll show below, when the intelligentsia-Party alliance broke down in the 1970s, the sites of communist authority such as the Council of Ministers and the Party headquarters became neighbours with some of the system's most vocal critics.

Location was not the only important signifier: the way in which a home was furnished might be an index not only of taste but of attitudes too. In the 1970s it was not unusual to see displays of empty beer cans where one might have expected bric-à-brac. If the 'meaning' of these mass ornaments eluded Western visitors, it would have been transparent to Poles. Beer was not available in cans at the time. Gaudy packaging of this kind was a metonym for another world where such everyday luxuries were widely available. Beer cans were not the subject of some kind of latter-day cargo cult: displaying these rarities suggested that their owners not only understood the West, but had enjoyed its tinned beneficence too. Described as badges of 'Engineer's Taste', these commodities not only symbolized desires but also the problem that materialism – of the most ordinary kind – posed to socialism. Just as the bricklayer had been a public symbol in the Bierut era, the engineer was a central figure in Gierek's dream of a Second Poland. (The prestige projects most closely associated with high Party ambition – in Warsaw, the multi-lane Łazienkowska Thoroughfare (Trasa Łazienkowska) and the Central Railway Station (1972–6), with its floating roof canopy over a huge glass box – were, above all, engineered structures.) If, as we will see, the image of the happy bricklayer who stacked the bookshelves in his new flat with the works of Marx and Stalin was a symbol in the 1950s, what might be made of his son who chose to put Heineken and Bud in their place?

If homes were sites of social distinction in rather veiled ways in the 1970s, their capacity to speak of the aspirations and tastes of their owners is unmistakable in Warsaw today. In a world saturated with DIY programmes on television and guides to stylish living, the idea that people can feel a close, even a personal, identification with the place in which they live is incontestable. One of the fastest growing sectors in Polish publishing in recent years has served the home design and decoration market. Practically minded titles like *Murator*, published for the large market of would-be self-builders (a common practice in an inflation-ravaged economy where few can afford a mortgage), and *Twój Dom* (Your Home), a glossy consumerist title, have tremendous appeal in a long suppressed market. It is not surprising that ownership of a home has become the most desired form of tenure in a city that has been subject to the force of privatization urged on by neo-liberal economists, as well as the demands of the World Bank. In the glossies this is usually represented by a detached house on its own 'exclusive' plot of land: whereas in reality the largest section of new home owners is made up of former tenants who have bought proprietary rights to their apartment (rights of inheritance and disposal), often at a discount, in system-built housing estates.

The official view of housing had been utilitarian and democratic in the People's Republic, at least in name if not in practice. Its living symbol had been the housing blocks for which Warsaw is notorious. But anomalies persisted in the socialist domestic landscape. While it has often been claimed, with some justice, that the large housing estates of the 1960s and '70s enjoyed a 'balanced' social mix with professors and street-cleaners as neighbours,[7] how did the thousands of private homes – many dressed with traditional details or made in the Scandinavian style with steeply pitched roofs and timber cladding – satisfy the ideological criteria of socialist housing? What social meanings were attached to their appearance in the city? Behind garden fences and kitsch ornaments, these private houses delineated the rise of bourgeois taste in socialist Poland. As I will show, they were formed, albeit often in strangely invisible ways, by the conditions in which they were designed and constructed. Today Warsaw's taste for domesticity, long hampered by the shortage of products and poverty of materials, is blossoming. New private homes are springing up throughout the city. What do they reveal of the new social lines being drawn in Warsaw society?

The home was sketched in little more than broad outline in the blue-print for the new society after the communists consolidated their hold on Poland in the late 1940s. One can identify important state-ments of policy, the most important of which was the *Sześcioletni plan odbudowy Warszawy* (Six-Year Plan for the Reconstruction of Warsaw) credited to the authorship of Party leader Bolesław Bierut.[8] Such announcements, for all their grand rhetoric, reveal little about the particular qualities of the 'socialist home'. His summary of the principal characteristics of the city's new apartments – that they should be 'comfortable, sunny, dry, aesthetic and adequately heated' – was hardly shot through with ideological elixir. At the same time, Bierut mapped abstract spatial dimensions with obsessive precision: 'the Five-Year Plan foresees the construction of 120,000 new homes of a total capacity of 12,000,000 cubic metres.' Not only did these calculations accord with the narrow terms of the command economy, as numeric mantras they also suggested the dizzying scale of the projects undertaken by socialism. This kind of statistical repre-sentation was a constant feature of official statements about housing during the People's Republic. At a macroeconomic level, it seemed that every metre of the new city could be accounted for; at a micro-economic level, 'sanitary norms' measuring spatial 'allowances' suggested social justice. In this vein, *Sześcioletni plan odbudowy Warszawy* was typical. It promised to end privileged possession of, and access to space. Bierut expressed the ideological significance of the new housing in terms of its potential to redress historic wrongs. No longer was the centre of the city to be the domain of the bour-geoisie: the 'workers' capital' was to be reclaimed in a great programme of social engineering. As if in opposition to the pattern of suburban drift found in the West, Stalinist planning claimed to encourage the return of the workers to the centre of the city to enjoy cultured lives.[9] Adam Ważyk announced the 'Return of the People to the City Centre' ('Lud wejdzie do Śródmieścia') in a widely published poem of the day:

To the chasms in the Old Town
Empty, blown up and torn apart,
On foot from the city's edge to the squares,
From the factories to the palaces,

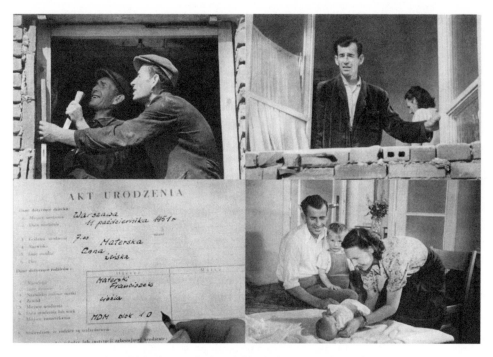

Anna Materska was the first child to be born to residents of MDM. Her father, a carpenter, was one of the construction workers on the scheme.

People return to the city centre
To settle along the length of the Thoroughfare
Along the length of New Marszałkowska's
Union of beauty and work,
Planning and prudence.[10]

Such poetic images were typically accompanied by the sentimental tableau of the bricklayer receiving the keys to a sunny flat in the very housing development that he or she had worked on. Here, were anyone to doubt it, was proof of the unalienated conditions of life and work in the People's Republic.

Often using reclaimed materials from the ruins, many of the early post-war housing estates in the central districts revived the dense urban character of the pre-war city albeit in the classical dress demanded by Socialist Realism. Three- and five-storey buildings were arranged around central courtyards. The ground floor was usually given over to shops, offices and other public services, while the floors above contained small two- or three-room apartments. As

Socialist Realist era housing estate built in 1952–3 on Anders Avenue (formerly Nowotko Avenue), photographed in 2002.

the years passed, the schemes of the 1950s grew in popularity among homemakers. Close to the centre and often set back from road traffic, they offer human-scale housing despite their association with the high period of Stalinism. Their solid walls, shadowy arcades and leafy courtyards offer respite from the extremes of summer and winter and their scale encourages a stronger sense of community than the later high-rise blocks to which they are usually compared.

The urban schemes planned and built in the capital in the early 1950s were crucial symbols in the Party's claims on authority. The new flats that rose from the rubble in the city centre were, of course, actual, material spaces inhabited by actual Varsovians (often Party officials, prominent figures in Polish society and leading workers, recipients of awards for their feats of productivity). But it was their symbolic value that was most important to the regime. Flats in prominent schemes like the Marszałkowska Dzielnica Mieszkaniowa (Marszałkowska Housing District / MDM), to which Ważyk's poem refers, were made into images for public consumption. These buildings were not only widely reproduced; they were

151

designed to produce 'politically correct' visual effects. The great adventure of building socialism was to be represented by massive and orderly buildings. Warsaw's new housing – often modelled on antique forms – was to lend added gravitas to the solemn task of building the future. Under pressure to address such lofty themes, architects sometimes let everyday matters slip. Schemes suffered from awkward spatial planning; rooms opened into one another without a corridor or hallway that might have afforded some kind of privacy to inhabitants; and supporting columns often disturbed domestic spaces.

The obsession with visual effects characterized not just housing but city planning in general during the Stalin period. Contemporary commentators often compared the self-interest of those who had erected buildings in the 'era of capitalist economy' in the nineteenth century (with their lack of regard for the aesthetics of the street and the city vista) with the vision of city planners in the 'age of socialism'. Edward Muszalski, for instance, argued that uncoordinated development before 1939 had 'spoiled' Warsaw's appearance.[11] It was as if the chimera of the collective city could be achieved by demanding visual harmony. Leopold Tyrmand, the novelist, privately objected to officialdom's shallow conception of space when he wrote in his diary in 1954: 'the city is not a picture' ('miasto to nie obraz').[12] Watching Warsaw rise from the ashes in its new socialist garb, he recognized that, in the Soviet-styled city, space was subordinate to images and effects.

With such heavy ideological investment in architecture, it is perhaps surprising that the authority had relatively little to say about the inter-ior. During the Stalin years, the domestic realm was reconceived as little more than a place where practical needs could be met. The value of a 'functional kitchen' was, for instance, emphasized to resonate with the mood of asceticism that the Party sought to promote:

> The new, bright and comfortable flats are not only a place of rest for the working man. They are also a place where one can work on self-improvement, a place where one may work out many of the ideas about efficiency that present themselves in the course of professional work.[13]

New homes, in other words, were sites for the reproduction of the new socialist citizen. The visual clichés used to illustrate these

The interior of a MDM flat, 1955.

reports included images of boys and girls reading and women sewing. In a public discourse that valued production, the new home was not to be a site of consumption where commonplace things were appropriated into personal, interior 'spaces' of memory and association. The socialist home was presented as another site of production alongside the factory and the office, where the material environment was disposed and actively designed to assist in the manufacture of a new self. In fact, early on in the reconstruction period, new apartment buildings were often allocated to entire professions or groups of workers from a single office. Colleagues would enjoy work and life together. In this way, the threads between production and consumption as well as work and home were to be tied together. Energy invested in the nationalized sphere of labour was unmistakably a contribution to Poland's radiant future. The relationships formed in this new world were therefore more important than the atavistic relations of friendship and kinship that had once held bourgeois society together. Like the places of work, the neighbourhood –

structured by government-sponsored clubs and unions located in the apartment complexes – was to be a key environment in the shaping of a new social ethos.

Although the ideal home in press reports was conceded as 'private' in the narrow sense of being the domain of an individual and her family, it bore no traces of what might be described as 'personality'.[14] Few unruly details entered into the frame to disturb the emphasis on the collective and conventionalizing virtues associated with good *character*, namely self-control and good conduct. Populated by generic social types ('everywoman') rather than named or identified individuals, these interiors inhibited any reflection on the part of the reader on the individual idiosyncrasies, personal needs and interests of their inhabitants. These new 'ideal homes' were not 'private' in Roland Barthes's sense of being the 'absolutely precious, inalienable site where [one's] image is free'.[15] In apartment blocks, residents' committees (*komitety blokowe*), an import from the Soviet Union, not only policed the residence but also sought to promote the cultural self-improvement of householders by, for instance, requisitioning books for a collective library.[16] Such voluntarism was usually and euphemistically described in terms of local 'self-management'. Here, it was claimed, was a premonition of the withering away of the state in communism. Voluntarism was, however, largely a euphemism obscuring the organization involved: the priorities and efforts of such committees were centrally set and conducted by local Party activists.

The extent of privacy was to be parsed. The socialist home required occupants without histories or property. Passage into the future was not to be encumbered with baggage from the old. The meagre proportions and limited facilities of the single-family apartment – the main unit of all new housing provision – was usually explained in terms of the new society being constructed. Leisure was no longer to be appropriated from the commonweal for private enjoyment, but was to be appointed outside the home for the collective good. Olgierd Szlekys, a prominent furniture designer, explained in 1955: '[In socialist Poland] we have changed the forms of our life. We have moved parts of private life to the houses of culture, to clubs and cafés, which are places to meet comrades replacing, we say, the old salons.'[17] In this way, the Palace of Culture and Science was to be home too.

The emphasis on good character underscored a series of practically minded articles entitled 'How to furnish the new apartment?', which appeared in 1953 in *Stolica* (Capital City), a fortnightly dedicated to reporting Warsaw's reconstruction. Most authors contributing to this series accepted the notion of the standard flat as a solution to the pressing requirements of post-war economy and, ideologically, the material expression of social justice.[18] Their reflections focused on the problem of how to furnish such apartments, for the pre-war possessions that most families brought to their new homes were traditional in character and 'excessive' in ornament. While these articles invariably emphasized utility and economy, they gave few practical clues to the eager designer, let alone the householder, as to the character of 'socialist furniture' (not least because demotic 'Functionalist' design associated with the pre-war Modern Movement was under Soviet prohibition). The ontological possibility of 'socialist things' – implicit in the materialist conception of progress – remained a matter of rhetoric rather than reality.

In one of these articles in March 1953 Stanisław Komornicki, for instance, alluded to a 'conflict' over interior space in the new Warsaw home. Staying well within the class terms of political orthodoxy, he focused his criticisms on the peasant citizens of the new city. Peasants had been welcomed into Warsaw as part of a symbolic occupation of the capital by the people: 'Socjalistyczna stolica – miastem każdego obywatela, – robotnika, chłopa i pracującego inteligenta' (The socialist capital city for every citizen: worker, peasant and intellectual). Yet in their small flats, according to Komornicki, these new metropolitans reproduced the social spaces of the peasant home. The small, often meanly proportioned, kitchen was used like the traditional *czarna izba* (black chamber) in the peasant home, a multi-functional room organized around the fireplace where household labour was conducted and meals consumed. In transposition, this 'disposition' in the new Warsaw apartment left the much-trumpeted collective services like the communal laundry unused. The other, *biała izba* (white chamber), which in rural life had been used as a site of display and for the reception of guests, was preserved as a space of display rather than of virtuous production or utility. The small, new flat, which typically accommodated a family in two or three multi-purpose rooms, was designed according to principles of utility. In effect, it would seem that the form of the apartment – whether newly built or salvaged from the old city – was disregarded by its inhabitants. In the view of this apologist for the new Warsaw, this trace of the peasant disposition in new socialist spaces 'was an unfortunate memory of long-past, unhappy times'.[19] What Komornicki had in mind was not the 'private' time of individual biography but the epochal conception in which life was regulated by the meter of progress. In this teleology, peasant life was destined for extinction.

HOUSING AS TECHNOLOGY

As the microcosm of socialism, the ideal home presented by the state during the first years of the new society was remarkably conservative. In fact, it changed little during the entire period of the People's Republic. While the preferred styles of architecture altered during the years that followed, with the Socialist Realist apartment block in the city centre being overshadowed by high-rise towers on the outskirts, the family apartment remained as the basis of all housing provision. The imperative to build remained constant too. In an attempt to satisfy demand, ever-larger estates were planned and built. By the late 1970s architects were designing estates for up to 160,000 residents.[20] Communal living, whenever it occurred, was a matter of exigency rather than ideology. While communal apartments – typically large pre-war homes subdivided by partitions for multiple occupation – persisted throughout the socialist period (still 12.7 per cent of the housing stock at its end), they became increasingly the subject of social satire rather than an instrument of social engineering.[21] Accepting the widespread attachment to the 'bourgeois' family, the Party sought to counter its conservative effects within the larger social unit, the housing estate. Here the collective would have authority and individualism contained.

High-rise estates reappeared on architects' drawing boards in the mid-1950s in the aftermath of Stalinism. At first as mid-rise schemes and later as tall point-blocks, modern architecture – despite the austerity of the design language in which it was written – was part of the Party's attempt to renew its contract with society. The 'return' of modern architecture to a city that had commanded the efforts of prominent Modern Movement designers in the 1930s (see introduction), was one of the most visible and widely broadcast symbols of the 'Thaw'. This episode is usually interpreted as an ideological retreat in which Polish communists moderated their commitment to

East side of Marszałkowska Street designed by a team of architects led by Zygmunt Karpiński, 1965.

Marxism-Leninism in order to hold on to power. Post-Stalinist authority sought to lower the ideological temperature by deferring to the technologically driven and efficient force of 'Progress'. By attaching its programme to highly visible symbols of modernization, the Party cast itself as a technocratic influence over Polish life. 'We have exchanged our fervour for ideology for a passion for rationalism' was its message. At the same time, the Party's 'leading role' was built on promises to improve the living standards of ordinary Poles. Asceticism, which had characterized much discussion of personal consumption in the first half of the 1950s, was abandoned.

True to form, Gomułka's new regime made a particular investment in modern building types. Numerous new homes were promised (though somewhat fewer built) in Gomułka's Poland for a frustrated population, desperate for living space and better conditions. The new Five-Year Plan for Housing announced in 1960, for instance, promised the construction of more than 75,000 new flats in the city.[22] New districts like Grochów appeared. With a population of 24,000 people, it was the first of a series of super-estates. For all their deficiencies in terms of design and construction, such schemes had a significant effect on housing density, bringing it back down to pre-war levels (itself a meagre baseline). Polish cities began a process of transformation, shaped by the numerous panel-construction, high-rise blocks for which the Eastern Bloc became notorious. The tall block became an important symbol of socialist futurology, endorsed by architects as the triumph of pragmatism.[23]

At the same time, the state flashed its technocratic credentials, promising to use the resources of the command economy to produce high quality mass housing. Bolesław Szmidt, a high-profile architect, charted a new relationship between architects and the state as well as the criteria used to judge new buildings, when describing designs for new twelve- and fourteen-storey blocks of flats:

> This work is mostly based on a 1960 decree of the Council of Ministers advocating the design and erection of prototype blocks of standardized apartments, intended for prefabrication and mass production. If a prototype building is found by a commission of experts to be progressive technically and economical in exploitation, then it is recognized as a 'type' and passed for mass production.[24]

In other words the architectural profession was licensed to experiment within a narrowly defined field of technical competence. Architects responded positively to the oft-repeated challenge to design buildings that could be built 'cheaply and quickly'.[25] The emphasis on efficiency enlarged the interest of architects in some aspects of the interior. In 1961–2 Maria and Kazimierz Piechotka, architects of Warsaw's Bielany estate, for instance, presented a typical scheme in which prefabrication was not only applied to constructional elements of the building but also to parts of the interiors. Designs and specifications were drawn up for standard kitchen and bathroom fittings that could be turned out by the metre and used in all new homes. While encouragement was given to inventions of this kind, the 'guiding' principles of sanitary norms (albeit based on an expanded per capita 'allowance' of space) and the requirement of family occupation, checked any radical social visions on the part of architects. In its modernizing moments, Polish socialism remained ever conservative.

The Party's claim to be engaged in the modernization of the socialist project was paralleled by a symbolic modernization of other aspects of the home. Numerous exhibitions promoted modern domestic design produced by state agencies such as the Institute of Industrial Design (Instytut Wzornictwa Przemysłowego) and semi-private design groups like Ład.[26] The interior schemes displayed at the 1957 Second All-Poland Exhibition of Interior Design in Warsaw and the 1958 'Exhibition of Contemporary Furniture' in Cracow, an early example of this trend, followed the proportions of housing association apartments. These interiors were furnished with proto-types that could be put into production by small-scale workshops, which the economic reforms of the period sought to revitalize. These objects included brightly coloured, modular storage schemes; rattan-seated chairs on spidery metal frames; and abstractly patterned curtain fabrics; each demonstrating their designer's

Cover of *Dookoła Świata*, 1957, representing a scheme displayed in the National Exhibition of Interior Design that year.

awareness of the latest trends in the West. These designs not only suited the new flats in their modest proportions, they corresponded with the patterns of life that they were to accommodate. Beds that could be folded into chairs, or storage units that could be used to partition space, were well suited to rooms that had to serve different functions and different users during the course of a day. While the new apartments were not 'open-plan' in the spatially fluid sense suggested by the Modern Movement in the 1920s, or in the ostentatious fashion advanced by American designers like Ray and Charles Eames in the 1950s, they nevertheless broke with the tradition of the inwardly focused, functionally segregated home.

In their emphasis on Contemporary Style taste, the 1957 and 1958 exhibitions of furniture and applied arts were typical of many such displays. Modern design was vigorously promoted at this time. Its merits were usually advanced by designers in narrow terms of utility and economy. But what of its relation to ideology? Were homes in the new style more or less 'socialist'? A direct parallel, for instance, might be drawn with the renewal of a modernist aesthetic in the Soviet Union during the Khrushchev era (and, in fact, there is some evidence that modern Polish design was considered strikingly bold there).[27] Party ideologues sought to find a new legitimacy during the Thaw by turning 'back to Lenin', that is to the roots of the Revolution, to rediscover principles that had been abandoned by Stalin. This was coincidental with a renewal of interest in the social and aesthetic vision of the Constructivists, the avant garde of the 1920s. Back on track, Soviet socialism, it was claimed, would draw closer to the collective life predicted in full communism. Domesticity, defined as private life and private possessions, would become irrelevant. The promotion of modern design with its emphasis on utility and technology, and with roots in avant-garde thinking, might be seen, therefore, not only as a refutation of attitudes to domesticity that had been encouraged during Stalinism, but as a step closer to the communist paradise – a world free of the friction caused by possessions.[28]

In Poland, while the aesthetics of modernization in the home were similar, the ideological shift that they represented was somewhat different. Unlike the Soviet Union, where a specialist design press aligned the Contemporary Style with neo-productivist discourse that invoked the avant-gardism of the 1920s, in Poland the aesthetic was promoted without reference to any socialist principles (bar the compulsory reference to economic prudence). In popular magazines it was usually placed within what might be 'proto-consumerist' discourses of taste and fashion. Interiors could, for instance, be described as 'fashionable' and 'colourful', suggesting not just design characteristics but, in their association with variety, social values too. In such exhibitions, the modernization of the home was not a 'project' in the sense that it carried an ideological imprimatur: it was far closer to what was described at the time as 'Refrigerator Socialism', the redirection of the economy to improve the supply of consumer goods (see chapter two). And like 'Refrigerator Socialism', this was a revolution of images rather than of things. Polish manufacturing industry, like a cargo ship, took a long time to change direction. For householders who wanted to demonstrate their modernity, the economy could provide only tokens. Brightly decorated coffee sets in organic forms and modish abstract ornaments, ubiquitous presences in the homes of young families in the 1960s, were symbols of unfulfilled desire.

PRIVATE HOMES IN PUBLIC SPACES

Although the material world continued to suffer from shortage and sameness, authority in Poland during and after the Thaw began to show greater encouragement of private life. Nevertheless, to make a home private – not only as a 'retreat' but also as an individualized space – was a challenge that demanded both economic and cultural resourcefulness. This was a task not only taken up by householders: it was accepted on their behalf by one of the most remarkable cultural products of the period, *Ty i Ja*, a monthly magazine edited by Juliusz Garztecki with a team of prominent artists and writers. First published in 1960, this 'glossy' (albeit in terms of content and layout rather than materials – for the cheap paper on which it was printed was rough, absorbing the ink like a cloth) was a phenomenal success. It attracted a large readership for its synthesis of high-brow culture from both the East and West with discussions of the material culture of modern life.[29] A typical issue might include a long article on the life and poetry of the Russian modernist poet Mayakovsky, set between an analysis of erotic Indian sculpture and a striking fashion collage plucked by the magazine's designer from the pages of *Vogue* and *Elle*. What was conspicuously absent from its pages was any discussion of the social or cultural merits of living in a socialist state. Each issue included a

Ty i Ja, November 1965.

regular feature entitled 'Moje hobby to mieszkanie' ('My Home is My Hobby') in which readers were invited into the homes of well-known writers, artists and actors. The word 'hobby' was a provocative anglicism, suggesting the home's capacity to function as a site of leisure and as an expression of an individuated taste and identity. These were the homes of actual people, even if they belonged to the

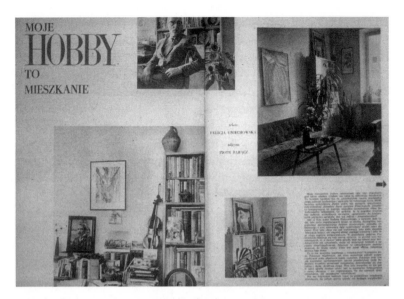

Stefan Flukowski's home as featured in 'My Home is My Hobby', *Ty i Ja*,
November 1965.

ambiguous social category of 'celebrity'. Hitherto, in the People's
Republic, this status had been attached to figures in the public settings
of political life or the workplace (even if that employment was in the
entertainment industry). By contrast, these *Ty i Ja* reports offered a
more intimate construction of celebrity. While many inhabitants of the
flats were stellar figures in Polish culture like Andrzej Wajda, the film-
maker, or the painter Tadeusz Kulisiewicz, the emphasis was on their
activities as consumers rather than as producers of culture.

Ty i Ja's articles tended to dwell on one issue above all others,
that of how to domesticate and privatize the modern flat. The relative 'placelessness' of the new tower block may have been beyond
the influence of its residents, but the indeterminate anonymity of
the interior was not. As a journalist writing about one of the interiors in the series put it: 'May I boldly announce: "Finally". Finally I
have an opportunity to present an authentic modern solution to the
functional interior and this type of regular urban flat of a standard
size.'[30] The 'problem' was so evident to the readers of the magazine
that it did not need to be articulated: it was how to maximize and
personalize the monotonous, meanly proportioned and badly lit
two- and three-room flats, the basic units of the new housing
schemes, within limited material resources (limits that reflected the

failings of Polish industry rather than the depth of pockets of the householder). The answer lay in clever organization of screens, imaginative lighting, multi-purpose furniture and so on. The notion that the homes of others could provide inspiration for the creative occupation of the standard flat could not have been made any clearer than when the editors launched a readers' competition in 1964. Prizes of money and consumer durables were awarded to the winners who furnished their flats with greatest invention.[31] Inadvertently, the practical limitations of the command economy stimulated a resourcefulness that *Ty i Ja* set out to tap on behalf of its readers.

While *Ty i Ja* recorded ordinary homes, most were the apartments of extraordinary people. Week by week, the reader was taken into the material world of the intelligentsia, a social group which had long substituted for the absent bourgeoisie in Polish society. This left-leaning 'class' had lent its support to socialism at the beginning of Party rule (not least because the communists lacked their own educated cadres), believing in the promise of social justice, but would become active opponents of authority in the 1970s.[32] In the intervening years the intelligentsia enjoyed the benefits of the official patronage of 'Culture' with, perhaps, a growing sense of unease. Moving on an international circuit of film festivals, lecture tours and art exhibitions, they had expert knowledge of fashions in the West and therein lay part of the appeal of these *Ty i Ja* articles to less well-travelled readers.

In their focus on the spaces and possessions belonging to the intelligentsia, the 'Moje mieszkanie to hobby' articles reflected on values that had been suppressed during the asceticism of the early 1950s. Old furniture, 'exotic' souvenirs and *starocie* (bibelots) were used to broadcast personal narratives: to tell of journeys abroad and family histories. Month by month, *Ty i Ja*'s investigation of the interior suggested the currency of differing and relative values and ultimately a conception of private life that had been contained during the Stalin years. In 1965, for instance, *Ty i Ja*'s readers were invited into the home of Stefan Flukowski, a poet and novelist. The opening passage sets the scene:

> Here . . . more than in any other example we can reveal the harmonic and peaceful background of family life. The banal architecture of MDM – the two-room apartment – does not

164

particularly mar the individual atmosphere of the Flukowski family home; a congenial atmosphere despite the design of the flat.[33]

In this account an MDM interior, which a little over ten years before could be discussed only in terms of public achievements, could be described in terms of a disavowal of the public realm. The tour of Flukowski's home allowed the magazine to sermonize: 'the best flat must be an individual one'. The flat was an extension of the inhabitant; an index of personality rather than of 'good character', the virtue so frequently praised in the Bierut years.

Left-wing by inclination (rather than by prescription), the intelligentsia and the *Ty i Ja* journalists cataloguing their homes made their prejudices against excess and ostentation clear. The axiom 'Less is more' was frequently proclaimed, though not as an assertion of modernist chic or austere asceticism. It was a demonstration of the judgement of taste. The commentary in these articles went to great lengths to arbitrate between authentic and inauthentic things and to attack the 'sarmatianism' of wealth display, a reference to the Polish aristocracy's historic attachment to luxury (see below). Repeatedly, the reader was told of the importance of resisting one's possessions. Individuality was demonstrated in the possession of attitudes rather than things. Like a number of nascent opposition views in the 1960s, this critique of consumption was somewhat to the left of the Party ideology. In fact, it was far closer to Marx's conception of commodity fetishism than perhaps any other pronouncement in the People's Republic.

While it might be possible to view these interiors entirely in terms of the wealth and taste of individuals, the particular way in which many of these homes were furnished with monuments to the past suggested social, even collective values. The patinated Biedermeier chairs, collections of vernacular spoons and dingy seventeenth-century portraits on display in *Ty i Ja*'s interiors might be best understood as symbolic apparatus, establishing lineage to 'national' traditions. What was represented was not just a domestic habitat but also what sociologist Pierre Bourdieu described as 'habitus',[34] enduring styles of life and 'dispositions' transposed across the generations. In other words, the apparent antiquarianism of many intelligentsia homes did not so much represent nostalgic tastes as ingrained ways of living.

Alongside romantic actions like uprisings and gestures like monuments, nineteenth-century nationalism had penetrated deeply into the home, lending high significance to apparently mundane acts and things. It was a patriotic duty to speak Polish at home when it was taught as a foreign language in Warsaw's schools. Just as the writer or artist was viewed as a voice for a deracinated nation under foreign rule in the nineteenth century, their homes and the possessions were – when they too appeared in the illustrated press of the period – often interpreted as symbolic reconstitution of a dematerialized Poland.[35] The antiquarianism of the homes of 'national bards' like Henryk Sienkiewicz represented not just a local variety of Victorian clutter: it was understood as an exercise in the preservation of a material culture under threat. The 'ideal' intelligentsia home was to be Poland in miniature or, as Andrzej Turowski has called it, 'un utopie rétrospective'.[36] Of course, the world-view of the intelligentsia in the 1960s had changed – existentialism substituting for romanticism – but what persisted were not only these material things but, more importantly, a set of strategies for responding to the compromised character of the public sphere.

The fact that these *Ty i Ja* articles appeared at all was a sign that the private (in the sense of that which is individual) enjoyed a kind of renewal in the 1960s. Not only was the private home legitimate but, importantly, this fact could be asserted publicly. *Ty i Ja* was, however, eventually closed down in the early 1970s when its cosmopolitanism proved too much for Gierek's new regime, being replaced by *Magazyn Radzinny* (*Family Magazine*). (The habitus recorded in this magazine survives to the present, albeit sometimes in forms that verge on kitsch. It is not unknown to find tower block apartments furnished in the style of the *dwór*, the traditional Polish manor house from the period of the Commonwealth, 1569–1795.) The anti-intellectual and anti-Semitic campaigns mounted by Party factions in 1968, and which ultimately brought Gierek to power (see chapter one), sealed the magazine's fate. Moreover, the rise of the Party's own educated elite, which loudly proclaimed its peasant and worker bona fides, meant that it no longer needed intelligentsia support. Gierek's regime made it clear that those with nomenclatura positions had licence to pursue their private interests and comforts. One of the most evident and, yet in some ways, strangely invisible effects of privilege was the creeping spread of new homes through Warsaw in the 1970s.

While great streams of words proclaimed the march of the tall apartment block across the city, virtually no effort was spent describing
the thousands of private homes built in its shadow. Private homes
were evidence of the 'good life' available to the socialist middle
classes in the People's Republic in the 1970s. Often screened from the
street by high walls and leafy gardens, their appearance and the
resources with which they had been built remained rather more
enigmatic. Walking along the unmade roads laid out in the wooded
exurbia of Zalesie and Konstancin, the favoured residential location
for the Party elite, one had the sensation of a visit to an affluent
suburb in Zürich or Munich. These districts were (and remain)
tightly packed with 'Tyrolean' cottages and Polish manor houses,
framed by neat gardens guarded by ornamental gnomes and
yapping dogs. Kazimierz Brandys described the spread of what he
called 'classless luxury' in the late 1970s: 'The entire country is blossoming with private residences belonging to the ruling cadres:
villas; parks; hunting grounds; complexes of buildings surrounded
by electric eyes; swimming pools; exquisite kitchens; the best
servants.'[37]

Although new private homes had first appeared more that fifteen
years earlier (often built by writers and artists, like those appearing
on the pages of *Ty i Ja* who enjoyed an income from sales and translation rights in Western Europe), most date from the Gierek era.
Under his oleaginous rule, the material desires of much of Polish
society were encouraged. High-ranking Party officials were not the
only ones to enjoy the trappings of the comfortable life (entrepreneurs in the expanding semi-private sector were also beneficiaries),
but their homes were often excessive or acquired by dubious means.
They provoked great outrage among ordinary people, particularly
during the rise of Solidarity in 1980–81 when anti-communist journalists recorded the abuse of privilege in the trade union's
newspapers.[38] Housing – the very issue that the communists had put
at the symbolic heart of their rule – became the field where the extent
of their moral and material corruption was measured.

When not offered as a direct incentive, new middle-class homes
required capital and resourcefulness (although small home-
building grants to erect homes on the edges of the city could be
obtained from the state from the 1960s and were taken up with

enthusiasm by architects in particular). These typically spacious and detached houses stretched the resources that could be acquired legitimately within the command economy. Homebuilders often siphoned building materials from the 'informal economy' and hired labour moonlighting from employment in the nationalized sector. Far from curtailing private home construction as a drain on the commonwealth, Gierek's regime licensed it in a 1976 bill designed to increase the number of single-family houses in the country.[39]

Following patterns of dissimulation characteristic of late socialism in Poland, these homes displayed uniquely peerel qualities despite their pan-European styling. Planning regulations, for instance, did not consider spaces less than 1.9 metres high to be habitable (and, as such, did not need to be included in the crucial calculations that measured the floor space). This measure was designed to allow for storage spaces like cellars. Consequently, four-storey houses could be described as having only two floors. After passing through the grand and expensively detailed entrances, with parquet flooring and stairs flanked with elaborate wrought iron balustrades, visitors might find themselves in the uncomfortably hunched spaces above. These domestic spaces were invisible in other ways too. According to official figures the extent of private home construction hovered around 10 per cent of all new housing during the late 1970s, though as most commentators note, many of these new homes were significantly understated or were not recorded in official statistics.[40]

High walls, deep shadowy eaves, smoked glass and raised, first-floor entrances made these houses doubly private. Not only did the luxury of these villas and smart terraced houses distinguish them from the standard, industrial forms of public housing, they offered shelter from the intrusions of the street. They were designed to protect their inhabitants not from the inquiring gaze of the state, but the envy of the passer-by. Although constructed with state approval, their middle-class owners and the architects that they employed were well aware of the disdain for ostentation and unearned privilege that grew in proportion to the spread of poverty in the People's Republic in the 1970s. Camouflage of this kind appears, however, to have become less 'necessary' in the 1980s. By the end of the decade the capital's suburbs had acquired some truly spectacular and exotic displays of ostentation (albeit often in the 'defensive' mode of the

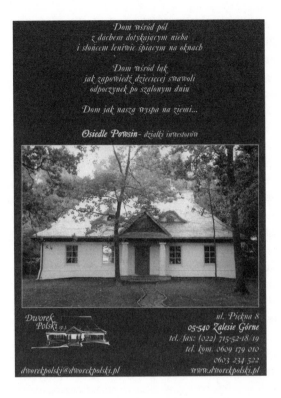

Advertisement for a restored *dwór* (manor house) in Zalesie in the suburbs of Warsaw, 2002.

fortress). Modern castles with tin-clad turrets and bogus rustication behind moat-house gates were an unmistakable measure of the riches that could be made – whether legitimately or not – in an economy in crisis.

The materialization of kitsch was given added impetus by the rise of Poland's post-communist *nouveaux riches*, an embryonic 'class' lacking a clear identity or claim on a common history. This section of society is somewhat amorphous, constituted by diverse interests including businessmen and women (many former apparatchiks who were quick to seize the get-rich-quick opportunities that came with privatization), politicians and criminals. Lacking a clear social profile and widely viewed as acting in self-interest, Poland's newly moneyed class has been the butt of humour and the subject of moral censure (much emanating from the intelligentsia, which has watched its social standing collapse in post-communist times). The uncertainties of social position and cultural identity are perhaps reflected in the schizophrenic forms of its preferred form of housing. The typical aspirational home in Warsaw is the modern *dwór*, a villa

169

based on the traditional rural manor-house of the *szlachta* (gentry).

A historic and rather indistinct housing form, the *dwór* has crystallized in the popular imagination as a long and low classical villa (usually in its eighteenth-century baroque dress – a prominent portico at the front under an overhanging tiled roof and a veranda at the rear). It has long been proclaimed as an authentically national form of domestic architecture, suggesting the slowly changing social order of the Polish countryside and the deeply ingrained traditions of the *szlachta*.[41] Much mythologized (and somewhat improved in the retelling), this extensive class was associated with the robust individualism of the Commonwealth (1569–1795), which elected its kings and accorded all noble citizens the right to resist illegitimate or corrupt authority. Unshakeable in his authority and sense of individuality, a noble was absolute master of his estate and his affairs and, in principle if not practice, the equal of all others who shared his rank. The vigorous independence of the *szlachta* lent the Poles a reputation for unruliness, much embellished by the uprisings against foreign rule in the nineteenth century. In fact, the *szlachta*'s robust defence of its own interests and scorn for government was, according to popular history, and popular fiction too, its contribution to national culture. During the nineteenth century, the déclassé *szlachta*, then sharing the misfortune of all, provided a model for Polish society. As many historians have argued, its traditions of equality, resistance and individualism provided the guidelines for Polish social and political thought and for a common self-image of Polishness.[42]

Revived in comfortable suburbs like Konstancin and Zalesie today, the new *dwór* is a facsimile of the traditional building form with modernized and luxurious interiors (often behind CCTV cameras and electronic gates). The luxury of these homes, evidenced by their saunas, swimming pools and billiard rooms, is a clear and unmistakable index of the wealth of their owners and evokes another defining *szlachta* legend, that of its sarmatianism.[43] As many popular films and novels attest (not least the much loved characters from Sienkiewicz's historical novels of the 1880s, which enjoyed a revival in the 1990s in such Polish movies as Jerzy Hoffman's *Ogniem i mieczem* (With Fire and Sword)), the *szlachta* loved to parade their wealth in extravagant possessions, as well as in bulimic bouts of epicurean hospitality. Furthermore, the traditional form of these new Warsaw homes reveals the dreams of their owners. The prestige that attached to the gentry survived communist rule and continues to prevail in a blurred social world where businessmen, politicians and gangsters rub shoulders and scratch backs. In this new setting, the appeal of the *dwór* lies more in its association with a way of life that resisted the intrusions of the state and its agents (tax collectors above all), than in its 'national' profile. Unlike members of the anti-communist intelligentsia who, as I have indicated above and will discuss further below, often treated their homes as an extension of the public sphere, for Warsaw's new rich they symbolize their right to exercise private interests.

PUBLIC LIFE IN PRIVATE HOMES

One of the challenges facing the majority of people living in socialist Poland was how to make their homes more private. This pressure was keenly felt whether one lived in a housing block where the sounds and smells of neighbours seemed to seep through the plaster or in a comfortable middle-class villa in the suburbs. A minority, however, turned the question on its head by exploring ways to make their homes more public. One of the earliest examples of this phenomenon was Miron Białoszewski's Teatr na Tarczyńskiej (Tarczyński Street Theatre), which he organized in his apartment in 1955 (moving to a new venue, an apartment in Plac Dąbrowskiego (Dąbrowski Square) in the late 1950s). Drawing upon a circle of friends in the artistic avant garde, Białoszewski, with Ludmiła Murawska, painter and actress, and Ludwik Hering formed a small company, 'Teatr Osobny Trzech Osób' (The Individual Theatre of Three Individuals). They performed fragments from the classical canon including works by Norwid, Słowacki, Mickiewicz and Shakespeare as well as Białoszewski's own plays.[44] Finding a grotesque character in everyday life, his works drew upon the language and experience of Warsaw's streets, finding absurd proportions in the most ordinary things. His dilapidated flat was dressed like a set with Białoszewski and Murawska producing crude costumes and backdrops by painting cardboard (matching the new post-Stalinist vogue for gestural and expressionist painting). It also furnished the props. If the drama called for a door or a dog, one was 'on hand'. It is estimated that the Teatr Osobny gave 300 performances to audiences that totalled over 14,000 people during its eight-year span.

Performance of 'Peruga czyli Szwagier Europy' by Teatr Osobny Trzech Osób, featuring Ludmiła Murawska, early 1960s.

The significance of the expression of public culture in ostensibly private spaces has to be considered in the light of recent experience of censorship and command. Polish theatre, like all aspects of culture, remained subject to the attention of bureaucrats despite the relative liberalization of the Thaw. While the censor's office tolerated greater freedom of expression after the Thaw, almost all forms of public culture still required its sanction. As many others have noted, the state's endorsement of avant-garde exhibitions, performances and publications (as well as the compliance of artists who ensured that their works avoided 'political' themes) neutralized art's radical charge.[45] Białoszewski is well known for his view that 'literature starts with speech and not with writing' ('literatura zaczyna się od mówienia, a nie od pisania'). In the first instance, these words might be understood as a statement emphasizing the poet's interest in the emotive power of speech. It also comments on the tradition of 'writing for the drawer', i.e. the decision made by a painter or poet to eschew publication or public display of their work. Art could be 'free' when it was produced for the narrowest of all possible audiences, the artist. Białoszewski's plays – despite their 'difficult' avant-gardism – were to be performed in public without compromise (although occasionally the company performed in Hybrydy, a Warsaw student club). For Białoszewski, theatre was a vehicle for a form of existentialism that stressed both the absurdity and the struggles of life. Teatr Osobny, as its name suggests, drew an intimate connection between art and existence, not least because it occupied the most intimate of spaces in the city, a home. In this sense, Białoszewski shunned the distinction between public and private that was being increasingly drawn by *both* state and people during the 1950s and '60s.

Other public uses of private space in the People's Republic were less concerned with the individual than with society. In the late 1970s intellectuals in Warsaw – figures who would ultimately become influential Solidarity activists and prominent post-communist politicians and commentators – formed Latający Uniwersytet (Flying University). This independent institution was, in fact, a revival of an underground organization established in 1883 by Jadwiga Szczawińska, which operated until 1905 when it was recognized and effectively incorporated by the Tsarist authorities. Without buildings or access to public spaces, classes organized under its aegis were held in private apartments in the city. Moving from home to home to avoid detection, the scheme attracted the support of prominent intellectuals, many of whom were professional academics at Warsaw University, as well as a wide cross-section of students (70 per cent women). At a time when Polish literature was viewed as subversive by both the Tsarist authorities and the Poles themselves, reading was claimed as a patriotic act. Self-education became a kind of national mania, strongly tinged with anti-Russian overtones.[46]

With typical historical self-consciousness, the opposition revived this phenomenon when the Association for Scholarly Courses (Towarzystwo Kursów Naukowych) was formed in 1978. With some subjects like the Katyń massacre under prohibition in university lecture theatres, the association's seminars offered opportunity for free speech. Favoured topics lay in the prohibited fields of social and economic reform and, inevitably, Polish history.[47] The response by the authorities to these assemblies was sometimes brutal, sometimes bureaucratic. Adam Michnik, later to be the editor of *Gazeta Wyborcza*, the main opposition newspaper, first published in 1989, was violently assaulted by a gang sent to break up his lecture in a flat in Ursynów in March 1979. On other occasions the state adopted a more orderly approach. In his book *A Warsaw Diary 1979–1981* the writer Kazimierz Brandys describes how the Civic Militia closed down one seminar.[48] Due to lecture in a flat in Bednarska Street owned by 'two members of the old intelligentsia', Brandys recalls being received by a company of policemen nervously smoking cigarettes and muttering into buzzing walkie-talkies, with clerks in attendance to record the details of the speakers and audience. Issuing receipts for requisitioned documents and checking ID's, Brandys characterizes the secret police as petty officials. He also places great emphasis on the preparedness of participants in the seminars to be interrogated and even arrested. While the seminars may have taken place 'in private', the Flying University took openness as a basic principle. In publicizing its activities and encouraging wide participation, participants in these seminars sought to refute the accusation that their actions were illicit or seditious. Being in the public gaze implied accountability and responsibility, attributes lacking in communist rule.

Discussions in ordinary homes were attempts to create alternative forms of public life. They conformed to Jürgen Habermas's definition of the public sphere as the 'realm in which private persons join together to exercise reason in a public fashion'.[49] While the German philosopher emphasized the appearance of spaces for middle-class association in the eighteenth-century city, such as clubs and coffee houses, in the peculiar conditions of the People's Republic ordinary homes played a similar function. Just as bourgeois clubs and associations nourished opposition to absolutist monarchical regimes, the kitchen in a tower block apartment or a spacious 'grace-and-favour' apartment in the Old Town, filled with antiques and books, was adopted as a place for dispute and dissent. From the idealistic perspective of Warsaw's intelligentsia, the society that formed in these flats seemed to have utopian proportions. Some years later, when Michnik and others formed their own publishing company, they took the name Agora, the classical Greek civic forum, a debating chamber in which views were expressed *ad hominem*. Adopting the name of this celebrated public space as the cognomen for their business – today the major media corporation in Poland – they signalled not only a commitment to free expression, but also to an open form of society.

There is no free love in a house made of concrete
Only married relations or naked debauchery.
Casanova is not welcome here.
Polish blues song by Martyna Jakubowska, early 1980s

As I have suggested, the ambition of architects and urban planners grew in the 1970s, massaged by the Gierek boom. They were able to pursue dreams of the radiant city, theorized by the modernist avant garde in the 1930s. From their lofty gaze above the drawing board, designers could imagine entire city districts (some the size of large towns) exploiting the openness, light and ventilation that high-rise apartments could offer, while maintaining the high density levels demanded by the state. While pre-war buildings and the existing infrastructure of central Warsaw inhibited the free rein of their imaginations, the suburban fringes were like a clean slate where expressive arrangements of buildings in the landscape – towering blocks above leafy bowers – could be realized.

In the 1970s five models of standard housing designs had official imprimatur and were adopted as the basis of most new developments in the country. Government offices like the Ministry of Spatial Development and the Central Planning Office laid down remarkably specific norms for architects and construction crews to follow. The amount of public art per square hectare and even the number of crane movements per 100 cubic metres of construction were specified in what became increasingly surreal calculations. The claims that these or any other kinds of housing represented essential architectural forms, matched to socialist life in Poland, rang hollow as the waves of enthusiasm that had been felt by the citizens of Warsaw in the 1960s died away. Once, when these buildings had been rare jewels in the cityscape, they had even been the subject of bizarre beauty contests with newspapers and magazines running competitions to measure their appeal: the fortnightly magazine *Stolica*, for example, awarded the title 'Mister Warszawa' to the most popular building. By the mid-1970s, however, the promise of technology was extinguished by the actual experience of living in large 'socmodernist' estates.

The charge most frequently levelled against such places as Ursynów, the largest of all and home today to over 100,000 people,

175

was that they were anonymous environments. Residents felt estranged from one another and disconnected from the city itself. These were, of course, familiar charges levelled at social housing throughout Europe. The main differences between East and West can perhaps be brought down to the matter of scale. The size and rapid construction of some Warsaw districts was remarkable and, for some, this was the cause of their sterility: Jerzy Szczepanik, chief architect of North Ursynów, ten years after the construction of what has become the archetype of the mega-estate in Poland, acknowledged the profession's hubris:

> The mistake was to entrust such a great task to one team of architects and to allow them to realize it . . . the method of putting up suburbs, estates, towns, buildings – like a home for one hundred thousand people – and creating a homogenous design like one great unit – this was the devil's idea.[50]

Constantly under pressure to meet housing targets, the authorities, together with the architects and planners in their service, cut corners. Social services like shops, schools and other recreational facilities set in a green and pleasant landscape, depicted in the picturesque drawings that appeared in the press, were usually postponed for completion at some later date (just like the red-letter day that would see the realization of full communism). Surveys of inhabitants of the city's estates revealed a correlation between the levels of satisfaction and their age.[51] The older the estate, the more likely it was to be equipped with the facilities needed for a rounded life. A child living in the city centre in housing built during the Bierut era in districts like MDM or Muranów was twice as likely to attend a nursery nearby than one living on a new mega-estate. Late 1970s neighbourhoods were often never completed: the lack of services added to the sense of disconnection between the grey panel blocks and the landscape in which they were built. Getting to the bus stop or the nearest shop involved a walk across a dingy wasteland of weeds growing on the mounds of rubble and earth waiting to be landscaped, avoiding the puddles and the broken paving stones .

Some commentators identified not material but moral shortcomings in the neighbourhoods produced in the command economy. While Polish sociologists – even during the socialist period – had much to say about the urban pathology of such estates, perhaps the

Stegny housing estate in 1977.

most enduring commentary was made on film. *Dekalog*, ten short movies by director Krzysztof Kieślowski and writer Krzysztof Piesiewicz, each drawing on one of the Ten Commandments, was produced for Polish television in 1988–9. Kieślowski and Piesiewicz's films were a gripping examination of Polish society in its most intimate setting and had a tremendous effect when they were first broadcast. *Dekalog* represents a world where petty-minded bureaucrats reign over those they are employed to serve and where even the most basic things persistently refuse to work. It is not perhaps surprising then that a cluster of high-rise blocks is the main stage for these morality plays. Although an anywhere setting for everyman tales, the location was nevertheless recognizable as Ursynów (not least because the district's only landmark, the Church of the Assumption designed by Marek Budzyński, with its striking entrance in the silhouette of a twenty-metre high cross, features in the first episode).

Most of the films deal with the upsurge of desperate emotions and chance events that disrupt 'normal' relations between family members and friends. At such moments, individual characters are presented with hard choices. Kieślowski and Piesiewicz's Commandments are, in other words, not dogma but a matter of dilemma. *Dekalog* 'Six', for instance, begins with the infatuation of a young voyeur, Tomek, spying through a telephoto lens on a woman, Magda, who lives in the apartment building opposite. When she confronts her lovelorn observer, offering herself to him, Tomek is convulsed. His romantic illusions are shattered and he attempts suicide. *Dekalog* suggested, at least on first impressions, an alienated social world in which people were turned into things and things seem to have authority over people.

The *Dekalog* stories were not only about social intimacy, they dealt with the spatial relations between people too. Adopting reflections as a cinematic leitmotif, Kieślowski used the windows that face each other across bare spaces of the housing estate to create not only a world of vistas and perspectives, but also of limits. As he stressed:

> Look through any window, there are people behind them. If you look closely, there is something interesting going on at their place. In other words, in the interior of each person you can find something interesting. You simply have to remove the mask, then we can remain together for a while . . . To have all the stories take

place in the same neighbourhood also had the advantage of always presenting closed spaces. The way in which those buildings are constructed and laid out limits the field of vision and this offered me many interesting compositions for the camera.[52]

The working perspective of the designers of estates in districts like Ursynów was almost invariably from above, the bird's-eye view of authority and of abstract concerns, such as the disposition of blocks in the landscape. Kieślowski explored a different set of horizontal perspectives – the camera often passes through windows to penetrate inside the apartments to the most intimate spaces of the home. In this, Kieślowski and Pieszciewicz encourage us to return to Barthes's theme of the 'publicity of the private'. Their conclusion was, it seems, that the damage done to society during the People's Republic – represented as the housing estate – did not result from the lack of privacy but from an excess of it. The neglect and blankness of common spaces was all the more apparent in Warsaw because it was in sharp contrast to the careful production of domesticity.

Privacy continues to dominate the domestic landscapes of the city today, more than a decade after *Dekalog* was broadcast, albeit in different forms. Much of the 'empty' land – once earmarked for cheerful schools and 'Pollena' beauty salons for the communities living nearby – has been sold to commercial property developers who have built new apartments between the blocks. Some districts that were once synonymous with social alienation are now in high demand, largely because of the opening of stations on Warsaw's single metro line in the mid-1990s. The planned and linear arrangement of the blocks constructed from prefabricated panels strung along the main roads leading out of the city has been disrupted by vividly coloured flats (more suggestive of Miami than anywhere in Poland) with pretty balconies, polished granite steps and private car parking. Even in districts like Stegny, built in the 1970s and where poor communications and the dense arrangement of the blocks limit the viability of commercial housing development, the signs of the times are ever visible. With wholesale enthusiasm for the car unleashed by hire purchase and the efforts of numerous car dealers, residents have taken to fencing off the land between the housing and the road to protect their precious mobile investments. And the appearance of elaborate panel doors, door-entry phones and security bars across lower-floor windows – classic features of the gentrification of social housing throughout Europe – testify to creeping privatization on the body of these one-time symbols of the collective society.

The first twelve- and fourteen-storey blocks made from prefabricated panels swung into place by tall cranes may have been important symbols of modernization, but they are growing old. While it was not necessary for architects and politicians in the 1960s to issue life expectancy notices on their creations, none claimed immortality for them. Estimates suggest that some have already passed their lifespan of twenty to thirty years and some may be entering the stage at which decay becomes fatal. How the socialist-era apartments age is an important issue for a city where the majority live in such blocks (56 per cent of the population are housed in the eleven largest housing estates). Built quickly under political pressure and often using poor quality materials, many are already showing signs of decay. It is not unusual for the joints between panels in the tall tower blocks to be alarmingly rent. More ominously, engineers worried about the flaws in the frames supporting these tall buildings have started to prophesize their collapse. Demolition without rehousing is only an option advocated by the most radical free-marketeers, such is the scale of the problem.[53] Piecemeal renewal of the kind made in Western Europe and in the former East Germany, such as recladding with heat-conserving panels, has begun with limited state support (although some optimistic clairvoyants foresee a time when renewal will be a profitable exercise if combined with new commercial development). The city authorities and housing co-operatives lack the funds needed to make significant structural improvements to the buildings or tackle the infrastructural problems that beset these estates. Moreover, Warsaw still enjoys a relatively mixed social pattern of residency and has yet to experience the flight to the suburbs that has resulted in inner city ghettos in the USA. The signs are, however, changing as the more attractive estates, well connected to the city centre and run by housing co-operatives keen to court more affluent tenants, begin to emerge.

While the European Investment Bank has lent the Polish treasury funds to finance urban renewal and energy-efficient social housing, and conferences are held in Western European universities to ponder the future,[54] the long-term prospect of high-rise housing provokes little discussion in Warsaw. It is low on the political agenda and hardly features on the pages of the professional and popular press. 'Social housing' – despite the fact that the right to occupy these co-operatively managed homes has been sold to the majority of their occupants – appears to be in bad odour, such is its close association with the interests of the old regime. Warsaw has repeatedly demonstrated its capacity for renewal since the 1940s. The task that it faces today cannot be greater than that which met those who returned to the ruined city in 1945, but the will – on the part of rulers and ruled – to engage with this matter seems to be considerably less.

Conclusion: Whither Public Space?

In the last decade a new profession, the security guard, has appeared on the streets of Warsaw. Black-shirted, crop-haired young men, shod in army boots, stroll sinisterly through the Old Town and hover in the doorways of the smart shops along Marszałkowska Street. Call into one of the new private housing developments and you will pass through a checkpoint manned by one of their colleagues. Who are you visiting? Are they expecting you? Enthusiasm for security is a product of the fear of crime that has risen palpably since the early 1990s. If estate agents are any judge of the markets they serve, the most attractive features of a new home for the wealthy have become security precautions.

Many people associate the freedoms that have been enjoyed since 1989 not only with a revival of dignity and democracy but also with crime and corruption. The murder of Marek Papała, the chief of the National Police force, and a series of Warsaw bank robberies in the late 1990s triggered the deployment of army corps on the streets. Warsaw is painted in the press as a city overrun by marauding gangs from the East. Describing crimes with an anglophone vocabulary drawn from American pulps of the 1930s, journalists write of 'hits' in shopping malls and 'bandits crossing the border'. The activities of the city's criminal underworld are reported with hyperbole: 400 gangs and an army of '300,000 well-trained and equipped criminals' are projected into its dark bars and shadowy underpasses. The latter figure suggests that one in four of the city's population is a criminal, an exaggeration that only seems credible in this economy of fear.[1] While the anxieties that such reports channel is genuine, it is combined with spectacular fascination. This is a point made by Juliusz Machulski in his 1997 comedy film *Kiler*, one of the most popular Polish movies of the decade. The central character, Jerzy Kiler, is a taxi driver mistaken for a hitman responsible for murdering more than forty people in struggles between gangsters. Imprisoned, he is unable to convince anyone of his innocence and so, when 'sprung' from jail by the mafia who want to make use of his skills, he adopts the lifestyle of a contract killer. He learns how to simulate membership of his new profession by watching Hollywood movies like *Reservoir Dogs* and *The Godfather*. Moving through Warsaw society with his new identity, Machulski presents Kiler as the only moral figure in a corrupt world. Everyone is drawn to him, or more accurately to the image he projects. Images, morals and actions seem to blur in post-communist Warsaw.

The extent to which there has been an actual crime explosion in the city is best left to the sociologists and criminologists. The obsession with the protection of private property that the security guard represents does, however, have some bearing on the themes of this book. Security is a matter that can inhibit and produce public space. To be able to move through a city's streets unmolested or to rest in its parks without fear of crime is a measure of the quality of public space. Moreover, for public space to be genuinely public, no proof of probity should be demanded of those who make use of it. A dialectic between individual freedoms and social responsibility shaped the opposition's civic discourse in the last decade of communist rule. In fact, the struggles against authority before 1989 (and in its diffuse forms since) can be thought of as conflicts over public space. This is not hard if one thinks of the choreographed rallies that the Party-state organized in the 1950s. They were designed to demonstrate the public occupation of the city by the working classes. Benjamin Nathans, writing about the public sphere during the French Revolution, presents a description that might equally be applied to Poland during the Stalin years:

> . . . rather than adjusting the public sphere . . . to accommodate society, society was radically tailored by a series of brutal excisions and exclusions in order to fit the mould of a fictitious public of abstract individuals . . . Behind the fiction of a unified, authoritative public opinion, an anonymous oligarchy thus 'prefabricated consensus' in the form of an ideology that acted as a substitute for the non-existent public competition of ideas.[2]

In other words, the public not only was spoken for, but it was reduced to a kind of representation of itself. In Warsaw, for instance, it was reified in the most literal fashion, frozen as stone images on the walls of Constitution Square. A bas relief representing the

Sculptural relief on the façade of a building on Marszałkowska Street by Franciszek Habdas depicting the citizens of Warsaw at the opening of Plac Konstytucji in 1952.

cheering throng at the opening of this new section of the socialist city on 22 July 1952 was carved *before* the historical event it purported to record had taken place.

Far from being the 'natural' terrain of the public sphere, defined by Jürgen Habermas in his discussion of the formation of bourgeois society as the 'realm in which private persons join together to exercise reason in a public fashion',[3] Warsaw's squares, parade grounds and shops were unmistakably sites of authority. Public spaces in this sense of the word were first squeezed out of existence during the Stalin years and struggled to revive in the years that followed. The indifference of most people to the common spaces of the city and the deep aesthetic and emotional investment that they made in their homes were both taken as signs of the collapse of public or civic values. By contrast, actions like those of the Flying University in the late 1970s were attempts to create public spaces, and society in microcosm, in the private sphere of the home. Likewise, churches – places which can hardly be regarded as open and common in the fullest sense – became public spaces during the 1980s when they opened their doors to the broad social spectrum that made up the opposition. For opinions and attitudes to count, they had to be expressed publicly and be disputable. With conventional public space constrained by authority, such alternative spaces were opened. Underlying such efforts was a conception of the city as a self-governing community in which citizens take an interest in their common affairs. The ability to come together to act together and debate collective outcomes was measure of the quality of public life in the city. Inhibited before 1989, hopes were high for a new *civitas*.

What should be made of the changes to the urban fabric since 1989? Has public space and the civic sensibility so desired by the opposition revived? The signs are mixed. Warsaw has become a more heterogeneous place. The busy thoroughfares, shops and markets have restored a degree of cosmopolitanism to a city that endured cultural and material monotony for too long. With the streets emptying after dark and the bars and cafes only patronized by tourists and petty criminals, Warsaw had little 'street life' before 1989. Today, on warm summer evenings, the centre is a busy jigsaw of pavement cafes, buskers and evening promenaders. Enterprising restaurateurs have set up business in barges moored on the river, in city parks and in the courtyards of the surviving pre-war tenements. The city authorities erect cinema screens in the grounds of the Palace of Culture for free screenings of films and stages for musicians on Plac Konstytucji to encourage life downtown after the shops have closed.

While Warsaw continues to be viewed as grey and homogenous by commentators from the USA and Western Europe, this is a matter of degree and perspective.[4] To those who have lived through its changes, Warsaw is a more diverse city than ten or fifteen years ago, both in terms of space and society. The large groups of Vietnamese, Turks and Russians who came as traders and now make the city their home have extended what many found a depressingly narrow social and cultural range. While it is true that they often coexist alongside rather than live with their Polish neighbours, any demand that a city should form a single community verges on the edge of dangerous intolerance. Heterogeneity can be the tonic that will make Warsaw a richer and more rewarding place to live. Spaces and buildings have important roles to play in this. The city's social housing estates have yet to become ghettos inhabited only by the disadvantaged and high-security housing typified by the gated community is the exception rather than the rule.

If the promise of heterogeneity is yet to be realized, the future of other aspects of city life already seems certain. Warsaw today has the atmosphere of a city where commercial interests have the upper hand, even in those parts so strongly weighted with national meaning. International corporations wish to be seen as the patrons of Warsaw's revival, drawing prestige by association with its traditional core. Citibank no doubt gained some prestige in the eyes of potential clients in the city when they sponsored the apparent reconstruction of the façade of the former Town Hall. In similar spirit, restoration work on the Old Town and Royal Castle – sacred spaces in the city's mythology – was funded in summer 2002 by Western European and North American corporations. In return for their gifts, they were given permission to drape colossal billboards across these buildings. The picturesque façades that make up the western and northern sides of the Old Town Square – the central attraction of the city to its small tourist market – were almost obscured by spectacular inducements to buy shampoo and mobile phones. At the same time the southern elevation of the Royal Castle became a frame for a long advertisement for instant coffee. While this kind of visual blight attracts some critical comment in the press, opinion seems to count for little and lacks sufficient force to curb the spread of this kind of pollution.

These mammoth advertisements illustrate the balance of forces at work in the city. Teetering on bankruptcy, the authorities lack the means to make significant improvements to the fabric of the city and struggle to maintain it. It is the pecuniary influence of business that holds sway. The millions of square metres that have been built in the city since the late 1980s have largely been at its behest. Private investors take little interest in the provision of new public space or maintenance of that which already exists. A shopping mall may be open to the public, but only in narrowly proscribed ways. As elsewhere in the world, the poor and the unemployed are not welcomed

Advertising on the Dekert side of the Old Town Market Square, summer 2002.

by the retailers or the security staff that they employ. Those who try to trade on the doorstep of these spaces – sometimes in protest at the attempts to control street trading – are quickly swept away by security guards.

Public space is not just a matter of access, as the experience of communist rule made clear. For a space to be fully public, it must be heterogeneous, tolerating difference and dispute. Freedom of expression is one of the features that links public space in a more concrete sense with Habermas's more abstract notion of the 'public sphere'. Today, few new building schemes in the city are open to public scrutiny in the form of architectural competitions, a phenomenon that perhaps surprisingly had some integrity during the communist era. Most corporations do not want to invite public discussion of their activities, not least scrutiny into the complex financial arrangements on which new buildings rely. To compensate for the withering away of public architectural practice, the city authorities and the Association of Polish Architects have promoted a series of competitions to plan entire districts under the slogan 'Warszawa Naszych Marzeń' (Warsaw of Our Dreams). Aiming to improve the coherence and identity of those parts of the city that are still marked with the legacy of wartime destruction and poor planning during communist rule, these competitions are designed to generate new ideas about the way to improve the quality of city space. Known as 'workshops' and offering modest payment for winning schemes, groups of architects produce designs with relatively few constraints. The results are publicly displayed, judged by architects and planners, and the subject of press attention. Their effects are less architectural than social, in that they create a forum for the exchange of views in an era when 'public opinion' can, it often seems, only otherwise be measured by market research.

In 2000 various schemes for Piłsudski Square – a windy place with high value in the memorial economy as the site of the Tomb of the Unknown Soldier – were published. The proposals differed considerably. One team of architects proposed exaggerating the memorial function of the space by covering the site with a bubble like a Victorian glass shade. A line of pine trees would screen off the ugly late modernist Hotel Victoria, traffic would be removed from the square by funnelling it underground, and the cross of flowers that had appeared on this spot following the Pope's 1979 visit would be resurrected. Proposing that the Square should also be the site of a statue of former President Wałęsa, a lampooned figure in Poland today, this scheme hovered on the edge of irony. Other, rather more sober proposals suggested reviving the proportions and scale of the buildings that had been on this site before the First World War in contemporary architectural form. The silhouette of the Saxon Palace, which today only exists as a ruined fragment, would return to the site in the form of glass curtain walls. The functions allotted to buildings in these ideal schemes – museums of modern art and council chambers – reveal the civic and 'kulturalny' values of the designers and planners involved. The merits of individual schemes are less important than the phenomenon that they represent. They will not, after all, be realized. The only actual addition to the Square currently under construction, the Metropolitan Building, a retail and office development designed by Foster and Partners, did not result from a public competition or a workshop. Nor will it be given the kinds of public functions that the city authorities and the Architects' Union value so highly. While the practical significance of the Warsaw 'workshops' is limited, they constitute an attempt to generate public opinion, an elusive and depressed force in post-communist Poland.

Exceptions do exist, at least on first impression. A case in point is Warsaw University's new library, which was built in the Powiśle district between the Royal Route and the left bank of the river in the

Scheme designed for Piłsudski Square by Pawlik and Partners as part of a Warsaw planning 'workshop', 2000.

mid-1990s. Somewhat optimistically earmarked for development as a centre of educational, artistic and cultural life, this area has long contained shabby warehouses and a prominent electricity sub-station. The busy stream of riverside traffic, which makes a walk along the Vistula an unappealing proposition, is being filtered into a new tunnel. In materials and form, the library makes a striking contrast with its neighbours. Suggesting a sweeping, classical colon-nade, the western elevation running alongside Dobra Street is formed by a series of artificially aged copper panels, each orna-mented with a text representing different fields of academic excellence: mathematical formulae, classical music notation and antique Greek script. This structure, which contains offices, is sepa-rated from the main body of the building by a long, glass-roofed atrium space. This arcade, entered from both sides of the block, is an ivy-clad interior 'street' with shops on one side and the library

The entrance to Warsaw University Library, designed by Marek Budzyński and Zbigniew Badowski, 1994–8.

entrance on the other . The library itself reflects contemporary architectural thinking in plate glass and cast concrete with much of the steel frame exposed. Designed by Marek Budzyński, the architect who proposed building the Temple of Divine Providence as a *kopiec*, the library also expresses his idyllic conception of nature as a healing force in the cityscape. Its roof, a structure which appears to merge with the ground on its northern side, is a park planted with long grasses and tough shrubs; meandering paths take the visitor into quiet corners and past running waterways. At the centre of the roof and looking towards the high-rise city on the horizon, one has the unexpected impression of a verdant Warsaw. Looking east, the view is of the wild banks of the Vistula. The grey city is truly green. This space is a remarkable addition to Warsaw. Moreover, it is public space, open to and used by Warsaw society (though it too is policed by one of the city's numerous security firms). People sit, read and meet there.

The green arcadia above the academy is, however, built on compromise in a literal fashion. To raise the funds needed for the library, it was constructed above an underground shopping mall, car park and cavernous bowling alley. Video games in the amusement arcades and neon lights promoting German beer flicker while the booming beats of Euro-disco echo around the bowling lanes. In a city that has had its fill of Marx, Warsaw University Library seems like a 'vulgar' lesson in one of his most basic theoretical propositions: that change and innovation in the superstructural realms of culture are always, in the final instance, determined by changes in the economic base. But then, of course, few are reading Marx in the library upstairs.

References

INTRODUCTION

1 The Polska Zjednoczona Partia Robotnicza (Polish United Worker's Party) was formed in 1948 when the Polish Worker's Party (Polska Partia Robotnicza) united with the Polish Socialist Party (Polska Partia Socjalistyczna). I have tended to eschew this long designation (as well as detailed discussions of roles and responsibilities within government before 1989) by writing about 'the Communist Party'.

2 'Peerel' is a neologism coined from the acronym PRL (Polska Rzeczpospolita Ludowa / the People's Republic of Poland), which has become widely used, often in the context of satire, to describe socialist Poland.

3 See Stephen D. Corrsin, *Warsaw before the First World War* (Boulder, CO, 1989), p. 13.

4 Peter Martyn, 'Emergent Metropolises and Fluctuating State Borders: Architectural Identity and the Obliteration of Warsaw in the First Half of the Twentieth Century', in Katarzyna Murawska-Muthesius, ed., *Borders in Art: Revisiting Kunstgeographie* (Warsaw, 2000), p. 141.

5 Piotr Paszkiewicz, *Pod Berłem Romanowów. Sztuka rosyjska w Warszawie 1815–1915* (Warsaw, 1991).

6 A. Słonimski, *Wspomnienia Warszawskie* (Warsaw, 1957), pp. 6–7.

7 See Edward D. Wynott, *Warsaw between the World Wars: Profile of the Capital City in a Developing Land, 1918–1939* (Boulder, CO, 1983).

8 See Ł. Heyman, *Nowy Żoliborz* (Wrocław, 1976).

9 See Helena Kolanowska, 'Varsovie functionnelle: participation de la Pologne aux CIAM', in Olgierd Czerner and Hieronim Listowski, eds, *Avant-garde Polonaise 1918–1939* (Wrocław, 1981), pp. 49–63.

10 Marta Leśniakowska, *Architektura w Warszawie* (Warsaw, 2000).

11 See Peter Martyn, 'The Brave New-Old Capital City. Questions Relating to the Rebuilding and Remodelling of Warsaw's Architectural Profile from the Late 1940s', in J. Mizołek, ed., *Falsifications in Polish Collections and Abroad* (Warsaw, 2001), pp. 193–234.

I MONUMENTS IN RUINS

1 Miron Białoszewski, *A Memoir of the Warsaw Uprising* (Evanston, IL, 1991) p. 16.

2 *Ibid.*, p. 55.

3 Milan Kundera, *The Book of Laughter and Forgetting*, trans. Aaron Asher (New York, 1999), p. 4.

4 D. Lowenthal, *The Past is a Foreign Country* (Cambridge, 1985), p. 210.

5 See Michael Steinlauf, *Bondage to the Dead: Poland and the Memory of the Holocaust* (Syracuse, NY, 1996); Feliks Tych, *Długi Cień Zagłady* (Warsaw, 1999).

6 Janusz Sujecki, 'Druga śmierć miasta. Przyczyny i konsekwencje', in Bożena Wierzbicka, ed., *Historyczne Centrum Warszawy* (Warsaw, 1998), pp. 190–202.

7 See Michał Bielewicz and Bogna Pawlisz, 'Żydzi komunizm', special issue of *Jidełe* (Spring 2000).

8 Michael Simmons, 'Jewish realities in a city of empty spaces', *The Guardian* [London], 9 July 1990, p. 11.

9 Sławomir Majman, 'The Hand that Giveth and Taketh Away', *The Warsaw Voice*, 22 August 1999.

10 Gutman, cited by Andrzej Styliński, 'Gehry to Design Jewish Museum', Associated Press, press release, 6 August 2002.

11 Białoszewski, *A Memoir*, p. 184.

12 Boy-Żeleński's poem '"Pomnikomania" Krakowska' is reproduced in Tadeusz Boy-Żeleński, *Słówka* (Cracow, 1954), pp. 301–2.

13 Cited by S. Jankowski, 'Warsaw: Destruction, Secret Town Planning, 1939–44, and Postwar Reconstruction', in J. M. Diefendorf, ed., *Rebuilding Europe's Bombed Cities* (London, 1990), p. 79.

14   John Hersey, 'Home to Warsaw', *Life Magazine*, 9 April 1945, p. 17.

15   Storm Jameson, *Journey from the North* (London, 1970), pp. 150–51.

16   On the symbolism of the worker hero see Piotr Zwierzchowski, *Zapomniani bohaterowie* (Warsaw, 2000).

17   Z. Dmochowski and W. Kłębowski in *Biuletyn Towarzystwa Urbanistów Polskich w Zjednoczonym Królestwie* (May 1945), cited by N. Gutschow and B. Klain, *Vernichtung und Utopie. Stadtplanung Warschau 1939–1945* (Hamburg, 1995), pp. 146–8.

18   See B. Szmidt, ed., *The Polish School of Architecture 1942–45* (Liverpool, 1945).

19   For an autobiographical account of one architect's work in the reconstruction of the city, see S. Jankowski, 'Warsaw: Destruction, Secret Town Planning, 1939–44, and Postwar Reconstruction', in J. M. Diefendorf, ed., *Rebuilding Europe's Bombed Cities* (London, 1990), pp. 77–93.

20   See Marcin Zaremba, *Komunizm, Legitymizacja, Nacjonalizm. Nacjonalistyczna Legitymizacja Władzy Komunistycznej w Polsce* (Warsaw, 2001).

21   On Party attempts to change consciousness see Marta Brodała, Anna Lisiecka and Tadeusz Ruzikowski, *Przebudować człowieka. Komunistyczne wysiłki zmiany mentalności* (Warsaw, 2001).

22   J. Kubik, *The Power of Symbols against the Symbols of Power* (University Park, PA, 1994), p. 3.

23   N. Bethell, *Gomułka* (London, 1972), p. 87.

24   B. Bierut, *Sześcioletni plan odbudowy Warszawy* (1949); trans. as *Six Year Plan for the Reconstruction of Warsaw* (Warsaw, 1951).

25   For further discussion of the introduction and promotion of Socialist Realism in Poland, see W. Włodarczyk, *Socrealizm* (Paris, 1986), and A. Åman, *Architecture and Ideology in Eastern Europe during the Stalin Era* (Cambridge, MA, 1992).

26   James Donald, 'This, Here, Now: Imagining Modern Cities', in *Imagining Cities*, ed. S. Westwood and J. Williams (London, 1997), p. 182.

27   Preface to the Polish edition of 1892 reproduced in Karl Marx and Friedrich Engels, *The Communist Manifesto* (Harmondsworth, 1967), p. 72

28   Adolf Ciborowski, *Warsaw: A City Destroyed and Rebuilt* (Warsaw, 1964), pp. 78.

29 Anon., 'Cały naród buduje swoją stolicę', in *Kalendarz Warszawski* (Warsaw, 1955), p. 199.

30 'Wkład SFOS do rozwoju kultury fizycznej', *Stolica*, 25 April 1954, p. 15.

31 See J. K., 'Warszawa na III ogólnopolskiej wystawie plastyki', *Stolica*, 25 January 1953, p. 10.

32 B. Węsierski, 'Ślubujemy', *Film*, 22 July 1953, p. 12. In this article Węsierski describes the 'Rally of Youth' (Zlot Młodzieży) that featured in the 22 July parade of 1952.

33 Anon., 'Waszawskie lipce', *Kalendarz Warszawski* (Warsaw, 1955), p. 157.

34 Åman, *Architecture and Ideology in Eastern Europe*, p. 119.

35 A. Turowski, 'Utopie et/ou rhétorique politiques', *Existe-t-il un art de l'Europe de l'est?* (Paris, 1986), p. 265.

36 Bolesław Bierut, *Zbudujemy Nową Warszawę, Stolicę Państwa Socjalistycznego* (Warsaw, 1949), p. 31.

37 A. Kotańska, J. Maldis and A. Topalska, *Warszawa i jej mieszkańcy 1945–1956*, exh. cat., Museum of the History of the City of Warsaw (Warsaw, 1995).

38 E. Goldzamt, *Architektura zespołów śródmiejskich i problemy dziedzictwa* (Warsaw, 1956), pp. 471–86.

39 Anon., 'Socjalistyczny w treści – narodowy w formie', *Stolica*, 8 November 1953, p. 2.

40 See T. Torańska, *Oni* (London, 1987), pp. 305–6.

41 *Stolica*, 22 February 1953, p. 2.

42 Anon, 'Odwiedziny u budowniczych Pałacu', *Stolica*, 1 November 1953, p. 7.

43 H. B., 'Najwspanialszy na Świecie Gmach Uniwersytetu', *Stolica*, 25 October 1953, p. 7.

44 W. Górski, 'Pałac przyjaźni', *Film*, 9 November 1952, p. 3.

45 Tadeusz Sobolewski, *Dziecko Peerelu: Esej Dziennik* (Warsaw, 2000), p. 29.

46 T. Konwicki, *A Minor Apocalypse*, trans. Richard Lourie (London, 1983), p. 4.

47 Mariusz Szczygieł, 'Kamienny Kwiat', *Gazeta Wyborcza*, 24–6 December 1991, p. 15.

48 *Ibid.*

49 Ewa Mazierska observes that the idea of destroying the building was deeply rooted in the social unconscious and was given expression in post-communist films. In *Rozmowy*

kontrolowane (Controlled Conversations, directed by Sylwester Chęcinski, 1992), the first Polish comedy about martial law, the Palace of Culture is destroyed. See E. Mazierska, 'Any Town? Post-communist Warsaw in Juliusz Machulski's *Girl Guide* (1995) and *Kiler* (1997)', *Historical Journal of Film, Radio and Television*, xix/4 (1999), pp. 515–30.

50 'World's Tallest Clock To Give Warsaw New Face', Reuters communiqué, 30 July 2000.

51 Jean Baudrillard, *America* (London, 1988), p. 56.

52 Ciborowski, *Warsaw*, p. 284.

53 Adam Zamoyski, *The Polish Way* (London, 1987), p. 239.

54 See A. Ciborowski, 'O udziale w pracach grupy "Stare Miasto" w 1945 r.', *Kronika Warszawy*, ii/38 (1979), pp. 31–7; 'Dzieje odbudowy Warszawskiego Starego Miasta', *Stolica*, 12 July 1953, pp. 4–5.

55 In 1937 the authorities in Warsaw had bought a house on this side of the square, the Kleinpoldt House, and two adjoining buildings, as the site of a city museum. The Warsaw Historical Museum was revived in 1948 and opened to the public in 1955.

56 T. Przypkowski, *Warszawa/Varsovie* (Warsaw, 1936).

57 D. Kobielski, ed., *Trakt Starej Warszawy*, Stołeczny Komitet Frontu Narodowego (Warsaw, 1952)._

58 R. Barthes, *Camera Lucida* (London, 1984), p. 94–7.

59 P. Ziółkowski, quoted in E. R. Chamberlain, *Preserving the Past* (London, 1979), pp. 8–9

60 Monika Adamczyk-Grabowska, 'My Warsaw is Gone ...', http://www.msz.gov.pl/ambasada/content/25_Warsaw_gon e.html [interview with Chone Shmeruk, 1997–].

61 Susan Stewart, *On Longing: Narratives of the Miniature, the Gigantic, the Souvenir, the Collection* (Durham, NC, 1993), p. 23.

62 Unacknowledged translation of Ważyk's poem in Edmund Stillman, ed., *Bitter Harvest: The Intellectual Revolt behind the Iron Curtain* (New York, 1959).

63 A committee dedicated to the rebuilding of the Royal Castle was established in London shortly after the war by Poles living in exile.

64 Adrian Forty, 'Introduction', in Adrian Forty and Susanne Kuchler, eds, *The Art of Forgetting* (Oxford and New York, 1999), p. 10.

65 Tomasz Urzykowski, 'Psikus mistrza Xawerego', *Gazeta Wyborcza*, 15–16 September 2001.

66 This discussion is indebted to Irena Grzesiuk-Olszewska's authoritative account of public memorials in Warsaw after the Second World War, *Polska Rzeźba Pomnikowa w Latach 1945–1995* (Warsaw, 1995).

67 Jerzy Jarnuszkiewicz, cited by Krystyna Prostak, 'Mały Powstaniec', *Gazeta Wyborcza (Stołeczna)*, 23 November 1994, p. 2.

68 Norman Davies, *God's Playground: A History of Poland*, II (Oxford, 1981), p. 36.

69 Poniatowski's monument has occupied this site since 1965. Before the First World War the plinth supported a figure of Ivan Fiodorovich Paskievich, a Russian Field Marshal, sculpted by M. Pimenov in 1870. This Russian monument was regularly smeared with wolf fat by Polish nationalists to cause Warsaw's passing dogs to howl. It was removed in November 1917. See Zachęta Gallery catalogue, *Figura w rzeźbie polskiej* XIX i XX *wieku* (Warsaw, 1999).

70 Sokorski and Jastrun, cited by Marcin Zaremba, *Komunizm, Legitymizacja, Nacjonalizm. Nacjonalistyczna legitymizacja władzy komunistycznej w Polsce* (Warsaw, 2001), pp. 169–70.

71 Neal Ascherson. *The Struggles for Poland* (London, 1986), p. 175.

72 Josef Banas, *The Scapegoats: The Exodus of the Remnants of Polish Jewry* (London, 1979).

73 Cited in Magdalena Opalski and Israel Bartal, *Poles and Jews: A Failed Brotherhood* (Hanover, NH, and London, 1992), p. 21.

74 Jan Józef Lipski, KOR: *A History of the Workers' Defense Committee in Poland, 1976–1981*, trans. Olga Amsterdamska and Gene M. More (Berkeley and Los Angeles, 1985), p. 42.

75 Timothy Garton-Ash, *The Uses of Adversity* (London, 1989), p. 97.

76 Janet Leftwich Curry, *The Black Book of Polish Censorship* (New York, 1984), p. 340.

77 On counter-memorials see James E. Young, *The Texture of Memory* (New Haven, CT, 1994), pp. 27–48.

78 Mirella W. Eberts, 'The Roman Catholic Church and Democracy in Poland', *Europe-Asia Studies*, L/5 (1998), pp. 817–42.

79 See Zbigniew Gluza, *Ósmego Dnia* (Warsaw, 1994).

80 Zbigniew Herbert, *Report from the Besieged City and Other*

Poems, trans. John Carpenter and Bogdana Carpenter (Oxford, 1985), p. 77.

81 See Padraic Kenney, *A Carnival of Revolution: Central Europe 1989* (Princeton and Oxford, 2002).

82 *Ibid.*, p. 160.

83 'Major or the Revolution of Elves', transcript of footage recorded in Poland in the late 1980s and screened at the University of Warwick in 1992.

84 Jerzy S. Majewski and Tomasz Markiewicz, *Warszawa nie odbudowana* (Warsaw, 1998), p. 82.

85 Nineteenth-century opinion cited by Tadeusz S. Jaroszewski, 'Sztuka i technika w Warszawie w roku 1870', in Monika Bielska-Łach, ed., *Sztuka a Technika* (Warsaw, 1991), p. 191.

86 See Olgierd Czerner *et al*, *Świątynia Opatrzności Bożej*, exh. cat., Museum of Architecture, Wrocław (Wrocław, 1999).

87 See Irena Grzesiuk-Olszewska, *Świątynia Opatrzności i dzielnica Piłsudskiego: konkursy w latach 1929–1939* (Warsaw, 1993).

88 'Wybrałem rozwiązanie nowatorskie' [interview with Cardinal Glemp], *Architektura* (July 2000), p. 10.

89 S. P. Ramet, *Whose Democracy? Nationalism, Religion, and the Doctrine of Collective Rights in Post-1989 Eastern Europe* (Lanham, MD, 1997), p. 110.

90 See Carol Rittner and John K. Roth, *Memory Offended: The Auschwitz Convent Controversy* (New York, 1991).

91 Miles Franklin, 'God, Honour and Poland', *The Observer Review*, 16 December 1990, p. 35.

92 Cited in Timothy W. Ryback, *Rock Around the Bloc* (Oxford, 1990), p. 16.

II SHOPS AND MARKETS

1 Gregorz Stiasny, 'Centrum wzdłuż ulicy', *Architektura*, 5 (2001), p. 42.

2 Padraic Kenney, *Rebuilding Poland: Workers and Communists 1945–1950* (Ithaca, NY, 1997), pp. 192–8.

3 This discussion of the Bikiniarze draws on Rodger P. Potocki's excellent essay, 'The Life and Times of Poland's "Bikini Boys"', *The Polish Review*, no. 3 (1994), pp. 259–90.

4 Leopold Tyrmand, *The Rosa Luxemburg Contraceptives Cooperative* (New York, 1972), p. 269.

5 Unidentified writer cited in *ibid.*

6 *Sztandar Młodych*, 10 September 1950.

7 Ivan T. Berend, *Central and Eastern Europe 1944–1993: Detour from the Periphery to the Periphery* (Cambridge, 1996), p. 84.

8 See 'Początek współzawodnictwa pracy', in anon., *Kalendarz Robotniczy na 1949 rok* (Łódź, 1948), pp. 216–24.

9 Anon., 'Polsce, prezydentowi, sobie …', *Przekrój*, 23 March 1952, p. 3.

10 Leopold Tyrmand, *Dziennik 1954* (Warsaw, 1995), p. 240 [entry for 5 March 1954].

11 K. S. Karol, *Visa for Poland* (London, 1959), p. 175.

12 See Zbigniew Landau and Jerzy Tomaszewski, *The Polish Economy in the Twentieth Century* (London, 1985), p. 206.

13 I. Witz, 'Nasz Plakat', *Przechadzki po warszawskich wystawach 1945–1968* (Warsaw, 1972), p. 53 [originally published in *Życie Warszawy*, 1953].

14 Stanisław Herbst, 'Nowa Historia Warszawy', *Stolica*, 1 February 1953, p. 13.

15 The pre-eminence given to culture was a feature of Soviet communism. See Svetlana Boym, *Common Places: Mythologies of Everyday Life in Russia* (Cambridge, MA, 1994), pp. 102–9; Catriona Kelly and Vadim Volkov, 'Directed Desires: Kul'turnost' and Consumption', in C. Kelly and D. Shepherd, eds, *Constructing Russian Culture in the Age of Revolution 1881–1940* (Oxford, 1998).

16 Norman Davies, *Heart of Europe: A Short History of Poland* (Oxford, 1984), p. 331.

17 See Anne White, *Destalinisation and the House of Culture* (London, 1990), p. 19 and *passim.*

18 Anon., 'Zamerykanizowany krajobraz', *Świat*, 24 October 1954, p. 21.

19 Catalogue to the *Pierwsza Powszechna Wystawa Architektury Polski Ludowej* (Warsaw, 1953), p. 59.

20 Jan Kurzątkowski, 'Sprawa mniejszej wagi', *Stolica*, 30 May 1954, pp. 6–7.

21 See Bolesław Bierut, *Sześcioletni plan odbudowy Warszawy* (Warsaw, 1951).

22 Complete data is provided in Stanisław Jankowski *et al*, 'Marszałkowska Dzielnica Mieszkaniowa', *Architektura*, 7 (1951), pp. 223–32.

23 Stanisław Jankowski, ed., MDM. *Marszałkowska 1730–1954* (Warsaw, 1955).

24 Rachel Bowlby, 'Supermarket Futures', in Pasi Falk and Colin Campbell, eds, *The Shopping Experience* (London, 1997), p. 97.

25 My description of this process is necessarily a brief summary. See Ivan T. Berend, *Central and Eastern Europe 1944–1993*, pp. 3–94; and Michael C. Kaser, ed., *The Economic History of Eastern Europe 1991–1975*, III (Oxford, 1987).

26 Tyrmand, *Dziennik* (1995), p. 50.

27 Leopold Tyrmand, *Zly* (London, 1958), p. 256.

28 Tyrmand, *Dziennik* (1995), pp. 254–5.

29 Unacknowledged newspaper report quoted by Stewart Steven, *The Poles* (London, 1978), p. 338.

30 Anon., '"Pedet" pod niebem', *Świat*, 2 September 1956, p. 21.

31 Bracia Rojek, 'Ciuchy', *Przekrój*, 9 December 1956, pp. 8–9.

32 Tyrmand, *Dziennik* (1995), p. 143.

33 When Tyrmand revised his diary for publication he introduced this term into a passage about the dress of the young in Warsaw. It has appeared in most editions of the book. See, for example, *Dziennik 1954* (London, 1993), p. 45. This term was adopted by Wojciech Lipowicz in a discussion of the applied arts in the catalogue for the 'Użytkowa fantastyka lat pięćdziesiątych' exhibition held at the Muzeum Rzemiosł Artystycznych, a branch of the National Museum in Poznań, in 1991.

34 Katherine Verdery, cited by Caroline Humphrey, 'Creating a Culture of Disillusionment: Consumption in Moscow, a Chronicle of Changing Times', in Daniel Miller, ed., *Worlds Apart: Modernity through the Prism of the Local* (London, 1995), p. 56.

35 Lewis Mumford, *The City in History* (London and New York, 1961), pp. 50–53.

36 Czesław Miłosz, *The Captive Mind* (Harmondsworth, 1985), p. 65.

37 Tyrmand, *Dziennik* (1995), p. 204.

38 Jerzy Wierzbicki, 'Parter ulicy w Warszawie', *Architektura*, 7 (July 1955), p. 198.

39 Jan Lenica, 'Le plus important c'est l'oreille', *Opus* (April 1968), p. 105.

40 Tyrmand, *Dziennik* (1995), p. 182.

41 Tomasz Goban-Klas, *The Orchestration of the Media* (Boulder, CO, 1994), p. 119.

42 Hansjakob Stehle, *Independent Satellite* (London and New York, 1965), pp. 209–10.

43 See, for example, Anna Bańkowska, 'Wiosna i kobieta', *Stolica*, 17 April 1960, pp. 2–3.

44 Barbara Ubysz, 'Handel zwycięża dystrybucję', *Stolica*, 25 November 1956, pp. 2–3.

45 Hansjakob Stehle, *Independent Satellite*, p. 172.

46 See, for example, Stefan Koziński, 'O projektowaniu obiektów dla handlu', *Architektura*, 9 (1960), pp. 360–62.

47 Józef Łowiński, 'Sklepy warszawskie', *Architektura*, 1 (1959), p. 48.

48 Cited by Grzegorz Skroczyński, 'Biblioteka skarg i wniosków', in *Karta*, 32 (2001), p. 131.

49 Katherine Verdery, *What Was Socialism? and What Comes Next?* (Princeton, NJ, 1996), p. 26.

50 Tadeusz Konwicki, *Kompleks Polski* (Warsaw, 1977). See also Stanisław Barańczak, 'The Polish Complex', *Breathing Under Water* (Cambridge, MA, 1990), pp. 163–71.

51 Václav Havel, 'The Power of the Powerless' (October 1978), in *Open Letters*, trans. Paul Wilson (New York, 1991), p. 136.

52 Grzegorz Sroczyński, 'Biblioteka skarg i wniosków', *Kartka*, 32 (2001), pp. 108–33.

53 Kazimierz Brandys, *A Warsaw Diary 1979–1981* (London, 1984), pp. 45.

54 T. Kovacs, 'The Spirit of Metaphor: An Alternate Visual Language', *Mobila*, 322 (1984), p. 17.

55 I am grateful to Mica Nava for introducing me to this idea.

56 Beata Pasek, 'Poland Facing Racial Diversity', press release, Associated Press, 28 September 1999.

57 As I write (summer 2002) these plans appear to have stalled over arguments about the location of this new market. See Alina Tobuch, 'Likwidować czy cywilizować?', *Architektura*, 6 (2002), p. 51.

58 Kate Connolly, 'Poles act against a second hand market threat', *The Guardian*, 2 July 2002, p. 11.

59 Marek Nowakowski, cited by Tobuch, 'Likwidować czy cywilizować?', *Architektura*, 6 (2002), p. 51.

60 Bart (pseud.), 'Przy kuflu o Konstytucji', *Gazeta Stołeczna*, 4 July 2000.

1 *Samorządna Rzeczpospolita*, cited by Jacques Rupnik, *The Other Europe* (London, 1989), pp. 166.

2 See http://archiwum.warszawa.um.gov.pl/kraj52/index (August 2002).

3 See European Academy of the Urban Environment website http://www.eaue.de/Housing/houswars.htm (September 2002).

4 K. K., 'Będziemy mieszkać lepiej', *Stolica*, 10 November 1968, pp. 12–13.

5 See Marc Garcelon, 'The Shadow of the Leviathan: Public and Private in Communist and Post-communist Society', in Jeff Weintraub and Krishan Kumar, eds, *Public and Private in Thought and Practice* (Chicago, 1997), pp. 303–32.

6 See *Warszawska Praga dawniej i dziś*, exh. cat., Museum of the History of the City of Warsaw (Warsaw, 1998).

7 Jens Dangshat, 'Sociospatial Disparities in a Socialist City: The Case of Warsaw at the End of the 1970s', *International Journal of Regional Research*, XI/1 (1987), pp. 37–59.

8 B. Bierut, *Sześcioletni plan odbudowy Warszawy* (1949); trans. as *Six Year Plan for the Reconstruction of Warsaw* (Warsaw, 1951).

9 The authoritative account of the principles of socialist city planning written to endorse Soviet practice was E. Goldzamt, *Architektura zespołów śródmiejskich i problemy dziedzictwa* (Warsaw, 1956).

10 Adam Ważyk, 'Lud wejdzie do Śródmieścia', in Stanisław Jankowski, ed., *MDM. Marszałkowska 1730–1954* (Warsaw, 1955).

11 Edward Muszalski, 'O popsutych Perspektywach', *Stolica*, 30 May 1954, pp. 8–9.

12 Leopold Tyrmand, *Dziennik 1954* (Warsaw, 1995), p. 233.

13 *Świat*, March 1953.

14 See Karen Hulttanen's discussion of these terms in 'From Parlour to Living Room: Domestic Space, Interior Decoration, and the Culture of Personality', in Simon J. Bronner, ed., *Consuming Visions: Accumulation and Display of Goods in America 1880–1920* (London and New York, 1989), pp. 157–90.

15 Roland Barthes, *Camera Lucida* (New York, 1981), p. 98.

16 See B-D, 'Wędrówka po Powiśle', *Stolica*, 21 March 1954, p. 2.

17 Szlekys's comments were made in a round table discussion recorded in *Stolica*, 3 February 1955, p. 2.

18 See, for instance, E. Tatarczyk's contribution under the title 'Standard Mieszkaniowy', *Stolica*, 31 May 1953, p. 10.

19 Stanisław Komornicki, 'Jak urządzić Nowe Mieszkanie. Artykuł dyskusyjny', *Stolica*, 1 March 1953, p. 11.

20 See *Architektura*, 4 (1980), p. 13.

21 Maria Ciechocińska, 'Government Interventions to Balance Housing Supply and Urban Population Growth: The Case of Warsaw', *International Journal of Urban and Regional Research*, XI/1 (1987), pp. 20–22. Stanisław Bareja used the setting of the communal apartment to great comic effect in his 1974 film *Nie ma róży bez ognia* (Every Rose has Thorns).

22 Adolf Ciborowski, *Warsaw: A City Destroyed and Rebuilt* (Warsaw, 1964), pp. 176–81.

23 See Waldemar Baraniewski, 'Odwilżowe dylematy polskich architektów', *Odwilż*, exh. cat., National Museum of Poznań (1996), pp. 129–38.

24 Bolesław Szmidt, 'Modern Architecture in Poland', *Architectural Design* (October 1962), p. 496.

25 T. K., 'O mieszkaniach optymistycznie', *Stolica*, 27 August 1961, p. 5.

26 On these design bodies see my '"Beauty, everyday and for all" – the Social Vision of Design in Stalinist Poland', in J. Attfield, ed., *Utility Reassessed* (Manchester, 1999).

27 The Polish novelist Tadeusz Konwicki recalled a party one evening in Moscow in the 1960s at which his hosts placed a great deal of emphasis on the fact that their modern furniture was Polish. See *Moonrise, Moonset* (London, 1988), p. 180.

28 See Susan Reid, 'Destalinisation and Taste, 1953–1963', *Journal of Design History*, X/2 (1997), pp. 177–201; and V. Buchli, 'Khrushchev, Modernism and the Fight against *Petit-bourgeois* Consciousness in the Soviet Home', *Journal of Design History*, X/2 (1997), pp. 161–75.

29 Accurate readership figures for publications of this period are difficult to ascertain. However, anecdotal evidence suggests that *Ty i Ja* was popular and disappeared quickly from Polish news-stands.

30 Felicja Uniechowska, 'Moje hobby to mieszkanie', *Ty i Ja* (January 1966), p. 36.

31 See 'Rozwiązanie konkursu Hobby-Mieszkanie', *Ty i Ja*
    (August 1964), pp. 33–7.
32 Maria Hirszowicz, *Pułapki zaangażowania: Intelektualiści w
    służbie komunizmu* (Warsaw, 2001).
33 Felicja Uniechowska, 'Moje hobby to Mieszkanie', *Ty i Ja*
    (November 1965), p. 41.
34 Pierre Bourdieu, *Outline of a Theory of Practice* (Cambridge,
    1997), pp. 79–87.
35 Beth Holmgren, *Rewriting Capitalism: Literature and the Market
    in Late Tsarist Russia and the Kingdom of Poland* (Pittsburgh, PA,
    1998), pp. 167–77.
36 A. Turowski, 'Les Utopies Rétrospectives: La Maison
    Polonaise (XIXe–XXe siècles)', *Existe-t-il un art de l'Europe de
    l'est?* (Paris, 1986), p. 179.
37 Kazimierz Brandys, *A Warsaw Diary 1978–1981* (London,
    1984), p. 105.
38 See Krzysztof Czabański, 'Privileges' (originally published in
    Tygodnik Solidarność, 16 October 1981) in A. Brumberg, ed.,
    Poland: Genesis of a Revolution (New York, 1983).
39 Although one quarter of the 382,000 promised homes were to
    be built by housing co-operatives, the bill endorsed the extent
    of private house building in Poland.
40 See Andrzej Basista, *Betonowe Dziedzictwo. Architektura w Polsce
    czasów komunizmu* (Warsaw and Cracow, 2001).
41 Marta Leśniakowska, *Polski Dwór. Wzorce architektoniczne, Mit,
    Symbol* (Warsaw, 1992); Maciej Rydel, *Jam Dwór Polski* (Gdańsk,
    1993).
42 See, for instance, Norman Davies, *Heart of Europe: A Short
    History of Poland* (Oxford, 1984), pp. 331–6.
43 See Maria Bogucka, *The Lost World of the 'Sarmatians'* (Warsaw,
    1996), pp. 111–24.
44 Miron Białoszewski, *Teatr Osobny, 1955–1963* (Warsaw, 1971).
45 See Piotr Piotrowski, 'Modernism and Socialist Culture: Polish
    Art in the Late 1950s', in Susan E. Reid and David Crowley,
    eds, *Style and Socialism: Modernity and Material Culture in Post-
    war Eastern Europe* (Oxford and New York, 2000), pp. 133–47;
    Miklós Haraszti, *The Velvet Prison: Artists under State Socialism*
    (New York, 1987).
46 Hanna Buczyńska-Garewicz, 'The Flying University in Poland,
    1978–1980', *Harvard Educational Review*, LV / 1 (1985), pp. 20–33.

47 Jan Józef Lipski, KOR: A History of the Workers' Defense Committee in Poland, 1976–1981, trans. Olga Amsterdamska and Gene M. More (Berkeley and Los Angeles, 1985), pp. 208–12.

48 Brandys, Warsaw Diary, pp. 140–44.

49 Jürgen Habermas, The Structural Transformation of the Public Sphere: An Inquiry into a Category of Bourgeois Society (Boston, MA, 1989).

50 Szczepanik, cited in Andrzej Basista, Betonowe Dziedzictwo. Architektura w Polsce czasów komunizmu (Cracow, 2001), p. 129.

51 Małgorzata Bartnicka, 'Warsaw Residents' Perceptions of Housing Policy and its Consequences', Journal of Architectural and Planning Research (Spring 1994), p. 4.

52 Krzysztof Kieślowski and Krzysztof Piesiewicz, Decalogue: The Ten Commandments, trans. Phil Cavendish and Suzannah Bluh (London, 1991).

53 Jacek Fiedorowicz, http://www.isl-projekte.uni-karlsruhe.de/isocarp_content/cases/cs01_5550/fiedorowicz1.htm (December 2002).

54 See 'Poland: EIB lends EUB 200 million for urban renewal & social housing', EU Press Release, June 2002.

CONCLUSION: WHITHER PUBLIC SPACE?

1 Marek Zieleniewski, 'When the Underground Comes Overground', Warsaw Voice, 506, 5 July 1998, p. 20.

2 Benjamin Nathans, 'Habermas's "Public Sphere" in the Era of French Revolution', French Historical Studies (Spring 1990), pp. 620–44.

3 Jürgen Habermas, The Structural Transformation of the Public Sphere: An Inquiry into a Category of Bourgeois Society (Boston, MA, 1989).

4 Joe Klein, 'How the Solidarity Dream Turned Sour', The Guardian 2, 12 June 2002, pp. 2–3.

Acknowledgements

This book has been a long time in the making. I first visited Warsaw in the mid-1980s when it had an unfortunate reputation for cold greyness. This conception has always been entirely belied by the people I have met there. Warm and optimistic, they have always been keen to share their city with me. The ideas in this book owe much to conversations with Maria Bartkowiak, Henryk Drzewiecki, Barbara Hoff, Zara Huddleston, Marek Kusztra, Grażyna Lange, Józef Łysek, Peter Martyn, Maciek Miłobędzki, Józef Mrozek, the late Piotr Paszkiewicz, Ewa Porębska, Milada Ślizińska, Jacek Skrzyniecki, Michał Stefanowski and Ania Steger. They are, of course, entirely absolved from responsibility for any mistakes that have forced their way into this text. I also owe many thanks to colleagues and friends in Britain and in the USA who have supported this project by reading drafts and sharing their ideas. They are Marek Bartelik, John Bates, Lesley Bisseker, Greg Castillo, Paul Jobling, Joe Kerr, Thomas Lahusen, Marysia Lewandowska, Katarzyna Murawska-Muthesius, Mica Nava, Susan E. Reid and Lou Taylor. And to the anonymous referee, who offered expert and discerning comment on the manuscript, I would also like to express my considerable thanks.

The British Academy provided a grant to travel to Warsaw as a guest of the Polish Academy of Science's Institute of Art in 2002. The assistance I enjoyed there was invaluable for my research. The Royal College of Art, my employer, provided a sabbatical which gave me the time to turn some rather unformed ideas and articles into this book.

The book contains images by photographers who have recorded Warsaw. Whilst every effort has been made to trace them and other copyright holders to secure permission to reproduce their work, it has not always been possible to identify and/or contact them.

Photographic Acknowledgements

The author and publishers wish to express their thanks to the below sources of illustrative material and/or permission to reproduce it. Uncredited images come from private collections or from the collection of the author. In some cases locations are also given below.

Photo Bruno Barbey (© MAGNUM): p. 77; photo: Anna Beata Bohzdiewicz: p. 134; photo courtesy of Marek Budzyński: p. 90; photo J.Y. Jones: p. 6; photo Edmund Kupiecki: p. 52; photos Henryk Lisowski: pp. 33, 116; photo © NATO: p. 101; photo courtesy of Pawlik and Partners: p.189; photo Tadeusz Przypkowski: p. 51; photo A. Rybczyński, © PAP: p. 177; Collection of the Muzeum Sztuki, Lódz: p. 107.